P9-DMS-726

# Recovering
# From Reality

## By Alexis Haines

Copyright © 2019 All rights reserved. No part of this publication can be reproduced or transmitted in any form or by any means, electronic or mechanical, without permission in writing from the author or publisher.

ISBN-13: 978-1-951407-00-1 Paperback
ISBN-13: 978-1-951407-01-8 eBook

For those who have been told that their pain couldn't possibly be real.

For those who have been told that they are too much.

For those who have stayed silent.

For those who have been silenced.

No longer.

Your pain is real.

This book is for you, this is for us.

To my partner Evan:

Thank you for all that you have taught me.

You helped to set me free from myself.

The gratitude is endless.

It's an honor to be your wife.

-Me

This book is a memoir. It reflects the author's present memory and understanding of her experiences. Some details, names and characteristics have been changed, events have been compressed, and dialogue has been recreated.

# Table of Contents

# Introduction

I put on my headphones and smile.

Dan Levy sits across from me in the studio where I tape my podcast, Recovering from Reality. That's right, it's also the title of this book.

Dan produced my reality show, *Pretty Wild*, which E! Network launched just as the Kardashians were heading into their third season, only a few short years after Kim was organizing Paris Hilton's closets.

I haven't seen Dan in years. And the girl he once knew has definitely transformed into someone else. It's easy to forget that, when you're the one changing—sometimes quickly, sure, but most of the time at a glacial pace. That girl I was before is usually a distant memory. So I guess I'm kind of surprised when, within the first two minutes of our recording, Dan hollers at me, "You lied about everything!"

He catches me off guard, making me pause for a second. Of course, he's right. In fact, Dan wanted to do a reality show about me and my best friend, Tess, *because* of those lies.

We were two wild party girls, pretending to be fraternal twins and Hollywood socialites, doing drugs and hanging out with celebrities across Los Angeles. We were super fun and also completely out of control.

And the whole point of *Pretty Wild* was that the world wanted to watch the train wreck that was our lives.

But Dan is also wrong. Because we didn't lie about everything.

We knew what he was looking for when he signed us up for the show because, though we were barely 18, Tess and I knew what all men were looking for. Sadly, we were also horribly naïve. Reality TV gave us the ability to continue living in our fantasy world. What we didn't know was how to live in *actual reality*. We embodied the pain and upside down value system of a traumatized society, one that is in rapid decline.

And I've spent the last 10 years trying to make sense of it all.

There are a lot of days where I can't believe what has become of my life. Believe me, I never expected to become a suburban housewife with two little girls, a dog, a cat and a husband I've been married to for almost eight years—that's nearly a record in my family! Most people probably figured I'd be dead by now (I was voted least likely to succeed at my rehab center).

And I probably would have been.

Except for the fact that one night, I was out with some friends, and realized halfway through that we were in the middle of breaking into someone's home. And the rest is pop culture history. The morning after

I got done filming the first day of *Pretty Wild,* police raided my house and led me away in handcuffs.

I was charged with robbing Orlando Bloom's home.

Nine months later, I accepted a plea deal, which sent me to jail. And then a few months after getting out of jail, I was arrested again, this time for violating my probation. I was a junkie. Did you expect anything less?

I was sentenced to a year in rehab in lieu of three to six years in prison. The choice was clear: get sober or die, girl.

I was 19 years old. I had been shooting heroin and smoking OxyContin for almost five years. I had been molested, raped, abused, jailed and on the verge of overdose too many times to count.

And like a lot of people in my position, I found myself looking in the mirror, wondering, "Who am I?"

Deciding whether to live or die is not an easy decision for most people suffering from severe substance use disorders, and it wasn't for me. I don't know if my hesitation was more about my indifference, feeling suicidal or the belief that it couldn't possibly happen to me. It was probably a combination of all three, leaning one way or the other, depending on the day or time. But that's where grace comes in. Because at the right moment, on the right day, I decided to get sober. And I lived (more about how I actually did this later).

But in order to grow from the girl I was into the woman sitting across from Dan Levy, recording my health and wellness podcast, I had to learn to love and accept that angry, traumatized, self-destructing mess that got me on a reality show, and made me an internet meme in the first place. What I realized was that, in order to recover from reality, I had to stay away from the limelight. I had to go out and start living a real life.

I had to begin to heal from all the trauma that had made me a hot mess in the first place. Then I had to learn how to build the family that I never had myself—one that is based in truth, honesty, sobriety and respect and the genuine belief that we each have our own paths, and that our jobs are to hold space for each other as we find our way through.

And none of that shit came easy.

Especially for a recovered junkie who used to panhandle for drugs in between shooting scenes for her own reality show.

And today, when I see everything happening out there in this broken world, it makes real life even harder. It makes me realize that the spiritual work isn't just about my own healing; it's about figuring out how we heal our communities, how we heal our world.

A lot of people still know me as the girl who left a voicemail heard around the world, where I yelled at a *Vanity Fair* writer for saying I wore Louboutins to court, when really, they were Bebe heels (I'm sorry, but there is still a big difference). And a lot of people laughed when I said, on national TV, that one day, "I want to lead a country, for all I know." As if a reality star could become the president of the United States!

But then I realized that the dreams I had when I was lost and young are the same ones I am working to make real today. Just because we are addicted and in pain doesn't mean we're wrong. Because our stories, if we heed the call to action of the hero's journey, can help us to show others the way out of their pain, and sometimes, in our own small way, they can help us to make the world a better place.

Because we all have the power to make our crazy fucking dreams come true.

And although I might not be president one day, I can still be a force for change in this world.

We all can.

In fact, as our world gets more complicated, more heartbreaking, we have to. We all have to be willing to stare long and hard at the choice: change or die. Even though, for a lot of people, that death isn't actual death, it might as well be. Our lives are often no way to live.

Being checked out of life doesn't make us any happier or any healthier, even when it looks like it does from the outside. It's fully living life, even the hardest parts, without a net that wakes us up.

So we can either stay asleep.

Or we can start to heal.

But I'll be honest. Healing is a painful process. It's scary. It's hard. It requires taking a really big leap. It's so much easier to live on automatic pilot and hope that things just work themselves out. It's easier to not care than to watch the news and then go and do something about it.

It's easier to buy the new handbag, the Louboutins, the Bebe heels, than to have to dive into the deepest, unknown reaches of your soul and figure out your shit. And we can still buy the new handbag or Louboutins or Bebe heels because fuck that, we can be both spiritual *and* look good. The difference is, we know our worth. It isn't in the material. It is in the eternal.

When we are able to embrace that deep worth within, we set right our society's value system. Trust me, I have helped contribute to the trash-ification of our culture, and I have been spat out of the belly of the beast with a story to tell about what I saw. What I realized is that I can try to make up for some of the messes I made by showing people how I healed from them, and maybe how they can heal, too.

Healing means feeling your heart shatter over and over and over again.

But healing also means getting to feel your heart.

It means having your eyes fill up with tears when you see a homeless person on the street.

It means seeing every child in the world as your own.

It means falling in love with your husband when you're in the middle of a fight.

It means loving enough to have children that can scare the shit out of you because you love them so much.

It means falling in love with yourself—even the angry, traumatized, self-destructing mess part.

My healing started in a six-by-eight-foot cell with vomit caked down the front of my prison jumpsuit, but it doesn't have to look the same for you.

Because we don't have to be junkies panhandling in Hollywood in order to recover from reality. We all get lost in our own way.

Some of us get lost to relationships, or jobs. Some of us get lost to our own egos or low self-esteem (spoiler alert: they're the same thing!). Some get lost in toxic families or to ideas that don't really serve them. Or to the pursuit of objects or stations in life that mean absolutely nothing to the universe, failing to speak to the best of our humanity. Others get lost in the idea that we are totally powerless—so what's the point, because we can't change anything anyway.

We all have our own prisons.

We all have our own rock bottoms.

We all have that moment when we look in the mirror and ask, "Who am I?"

And we all have that moment when we remember how far we've come.

And how far we have yet to go.

But I promise you; we can get there. Especially if we do it together.

Every day, people I've never met send me stories on Instagram. Those stories have both broken my heart and given me the deepest and most profound inspiration. Know this, you help me as much as I could ever help you.

Because whether you know me from the podcast or my Instagram or that voicemail from a broken girl, we're all part of the same tribe. We're all here to heal.

So let's do it. Let's recover from reality…together.

## Chapter One

# And So It Is

*"You own everything that happened to you.*
*Tell your stories. If people wanted you to write warmly*
*about them, they should have behaved better."*
*—Anne Lamont*

I'm constantly amazed by life's mysteries. How we got here and what magical force makes us into living, breathing humans. Who or what are we? These questions fascinate me. My mom raised me to believe in fates and fairies and a bunch of woo-woo shit that now fills multiple accounts on Instagram. I personally still have no idea how this whole universe works. All I know for sure is that I experienced a real miracle in my recovery. This is what I learned: somehow, when we accept the unknown and surrender to the process, if everything else lines up perfectly in that moment, we can change our destiny and own our lives.

I owe my whole life to a random Showtime series called *Brothers*. Because without all the twists and turns that make a TV show a TV show, without the green light and staffing, without the chance occurrence of my dad landing a gig as Director of Photography, and my mom snagging a guest spot on an episode, I wouldn't be here right now. Neither would my sister, Gabby.

We were born in the shadows of Hollywood. If you don't know anything about Hollywood, it's the place where everyone is chasing something and very few catch it, never finding what they thought they were looking for in the first place.

We were born in Calabasas, a quiet bedroom community about 30 miles east of Los Angeles, before the Kardashians and Drake made it famous, and grew up a stone's throw away, in Westlake Village, California. After my parents split when I was three years old, we always looked like we had more than we actually did.

Because looking good meant everything. I vividly recall my mom doing her makeup while driving us to church one morning, telling us, "Sometimes beauty is pain." It's a miracle she never crashed the car. She was always dressed to the nines, with the flawless appearance of a porcelain doll, and her two perfectly dressed munchkins in the back seat.

My mom moved out to Los Angeles from Chicago to become an actress. She modeled in Japan when she was younger and landed herself in the pages of the South American edition of *Playboy*. She was beautiful and outgoing and the kind of woman that attracted attention wherever she went. She was proud of this attractiveness and probably derived a lot of power from it, which I'm sure made it all the more painful when she found out that my father was cheating on her.

My dad had a bad problem with secrets and lies. He told women that he and my mom were separated when they were still very much together, legally and otherwise. According to my mom, their relationship was a lot of fun in the beginning, but by the time he found a younger, blonder woman to date, she was already exhausted by his using and drinking.

Hollywood is all about getting high. It's all about that huge dopamine hit you get when you land the part or sign the deal. It's all about getting the phone call that will change your life. They say there's no such thing as a bad meeting in Hollywood. Everyone is blowing sunshine up everyone else's ass, even, and maybe especially, when they have no intention of delivering anything. And now we even have the DM that will take you from nowhere to influencer in 50,000 followers. We're all chasing something to make ourselves feel better.

My dad chased booze and women and drugs. My mom chased spirituality and fame. Which sounds like a weird combo—but my mom really believed that if we were just given a bigger shot in this world, we could make it a better place. I get it. I guess in addition to fates and fairies, I still believe in that too. She never believed fame was an end; she believed it was the path to a better life.

But my mom's expectations always overshot reality.

She thought that she would come to Los Angeles and become a major star, but the closest she got was a part on *The Nanny* and a few other minor gigs. She thought she would marry my father and they would become some Hollywood power couple. What she got was a cheating drunk who was on to his next marriage before he was done with theirs.

When things didn't work out for her, she turned her attentions to Gabby and me.

I'll say right now, it isn't easy to tell these truths about my mom, or my dad for that matter.

Our stories are the one thing we have when we can't trust anything else. They might be dark, but in them is our truth. And truth is always our light. I find compassion for my mom, however challenging that is sometimes, because I know how she was raised, and how her parents were raised.

An entire generation of parents was given the perfect excuse from their self-help gurus, hiding behind the mantra, "We did the best we could with the tools we had." Like my good friend Bob Forrest told me after personally witnessing my mom contort herself into a human pretzel trying to put this rationalization to work, "No she didn't."

Because it's often the truth for these parents. They didn't. My mom could have gone back to school. She could have gone to therapy. She could have made better choices. And my dad? He could have gotten sober. He could have grown up and been the responsible, caring adult we needed him to be.

Today, I see both the good and bad that my parents did. Though I have compassion for them, I also know that when I look at my own daughters, I am willing to dedicate the time, energy and resources to doing so much better. I am willing to take full responsibility for how I raise them, for good or ill. Parents can hide behind the excuse of the times or their own addictions and narcissisms, but they also fucked up. And that's okay, as long as we know the difference. Gabby and I deserved a lot more than we got. And we've both spent the last 10 years working to heal those little girls inside who didn't get what they deserved, who weren't protected and honored the way my husband, Evan, and I work to protect and honor our own daughters.

But back in 1995, when my father was getting remarried and my mother was smoking pot 24/7, nobody was paying much attention to the two little girls in the middle. So Gabby and I just learned to survive. And we saw that if you wanted to survive as a girl in America, you'd better look cute doing it. We took dance lessons and practiced being pretty. We were constantly told to "act like little ladies."

My mom never went to college, and much like her, I wasn't very good in school. Though I have a love for learning new things, I think that all the chaos at home distracted me from my ability to do well in class as a kid. My mom was always all over the place, meaning we often made it to school late, and our homework was almost never completed.

I grew up thinking that beauty was always more important than brains, until I found out that beauty could only take you so far, and usually not where you wanted to go, anyway.

I was five years old when my mom met another mom who liked to smoke pot.

Tracie was a stunning woman with long painted nails, an arm full of bangle bracelets and wild blonde hair. She had a big tattoo of an angel on her stomach. She used to joke that she wanted to slap a nipple on a bottle of Vodka and go to sleep, a story she loves to share, and still laughs about every time. Tracie also had a daughter, Tess, who was a year older than me. And so our moms quickly became friends.

My mom and Tracie would spend hours in our garage, smoking pot and doing crafts, making us jewelry and hair clips, thinking they were these model mothers, when really; they were more like teenagers playacting as adults. Tess quickly joined Gabby and I as our third sister, which is how we referred to each other for years.

"Are you two twins?" I still remember the excited look on the man's face as he asked Tess and I the same question so many men would ask us over the years. We were only eight and nine, and yet I could see he wanted something from us.

It's ironic that Tess and I would come to star on a show called *Pretty Wild*, because we had been pretty and wild since we were kids. We were feral, surviving on our own for the most part, raising each other. Though I had my mom, and Tess had her family, there was something about our lives that always made us feel like we were kids in the wild. We were untamed, unfit, as much as my mom tried to make us look like normal, pretty little girls. Other people could sense it—particularly a certain type of man—even though we were only children.

From the start, it felt like Tess and I attracted the same attention that I had watched my mother receive. People noticed us when we walked into restaurants or stores. Women complimented, "They're so pretty." Men commented, "They're so pretty." I could feel the difference. On our own, we might have gotten some attention, but together, it was double trouble. My mom also saw it, enrolling us in dance classes, convinced we could be child stars.

Then Tess' life blew up as her mom struggled with her own issues. Though my mom liked to party, she was a functioning parent. We might have been late to school, but we got there. My mom would get hyperfocused on diets and fads. She was into Keto and Paleo and sage and oils before anyone was even talking like that. She would do energy cleanses, and pagan rituals. But she was so focused on self-realization, she often forgot about us.

In comparison, Tess bounced from one friend's house to the next; including a boy she met in school, Nick Prugo. Tess and Nick actually went to rehab together when they were just teenagers (but more on Nick and the Bling Ring later).

For a long time, she lived with us. Tess, Gabby and I became inseparable. We went everywhere together, did everything together.

Throughout my early years, my mom had a series of boyfriends; men we hoped would become our new daddies. And some of them would have been great at the job. But then there would be a breakup and my mom would be devastated. And we would have lost another father. When I was 12 years old, she eventually remarried. By that time, I refused to call anyone dad.

Something happens when you don't have any men you can trust in your life. Something about partnerships, love and faith gets thoroughly shaken. I grew up believing that men would always leave, that they couldn't be counted on. And I didn't see much better from women. Through my mom and Tess, I learned that women could be your friend one minute, and your enemy the next. I was just a child, and I already believed I couldn't trust anyone. And if I couldn't trust the people who were supposed to love me, how could I trust any source of love in the universe? How could I have any faith?

It was the early 2000s, and Tess, Gabby and I watched Britney Spears, Christina Aguilera and Shakira, and believed that if we just learned how to shake our hips right, we wouldn't have to worry about how to pay the bills. This was going to be important, we thought. Because we were becoming poorer and poorer while we were ironically living a stone's throw away from where Kris and Bruce Jenner were raising a brood of rich and pretty girls.

At first, my dad paid alimony and child support. But by the time I was 11, he had already ruined the marriage he left my mom for—with a woman we had all come to love and trust as another mother. Once my dad's money began to dry up, my mom wasn't quite sure how to keep up. We were always the poor kids living in the rich neighborhoods. We would be at TJ Maxx and thrift shops while our friends from school were shopping at Barneys and Nordstrom. Money was a constant source of anxiety in our house. Running out of toilet paper was normal, and one Christmas where we wrapped our old toys because we couldn't afford new ones.

I know this is the reality for a lot of Americans and a lot of people around the world, but it wasn't something we ever learned to embrace. We were taught to portray these other identities, to try and fit in with our wealthy neighbors.

And that lie was the worst part of it.

My mom was too embarrassed to get food stamps. Instead, she made my dad give his to her. I'm not quite sure how we were able to eat during that time. Not only would my mom not go to the social security office to get an EBT card, she also wouldn't go into the grocery store to use it. Instead, she had Gabby and I do the shopping. My mom never planned for a life where she wasn't being taken care of financially. A lot of that began to fall to me. I got my first job when I was 14. I washed dishes at a local coffee shop from

4:30 am to 1 pm, and then babysat neighborhood kids for the rest of the day, because my mom needed money.

She became determined to rewrite the script of her life. She had been waiting for Prince Charming to come save us. Then she realized she had something even more powerful in her grasp. She had three princesses, just waiting for their tiaras. My mom convinced all of us that as long as we did what she said, we were going to become what she had failed to be—stars. I didn't really know what that meant, but I knew that I didn't want to feel like the kid who couldn't keep up. School was already hard enough. And I really wanted to believe there was a way out. So I began to believe in my mother's dream, and that the fates and the fairies that she prayed to could make everything better.

One thing my mom did get right—and that I am super grateful for today—is the belief that we are all here with a divine purpose. Whether that means helping people in really big ways or just by small acts of kindness, we are all here to grow in love and faith. Sometimes the road to that purpose is hard, sometimes it's heartbreaking, but once we find that space and recognize that we are here for an important and miraculous reason, we can begin to believe in something bigger than ourselves. That's the space where healing starts.

Unfortunately, most of us are in need of healing. Because for many, life is filled with pain and trauma, it is marked by loneliness and disconnection. I have learned we can either stay in the cycle of intergenerational trauma and end up trapped, or we can find our way out.

But first, we have to be willing to go through it.

-----------------------------------------------------------

## Chapter Two

# The Monster

*"Violators cannot live with the truth: survivors cannot live without it. But the truth won't go away. It will keep surfacing until it is recognized. Truth will outlast any campaigns mounted against it, no matter how mighty, clever, or long. It is invincible."*
—Chrystine Oksana

I always knew it happened. Hazy memories of a wedding, a hotel room, being told it was all just a game. It wasn't until I got sober that I remembered the rest. I'll offer you a trigger warning right now. I am going to tell you details regarding childhood sexual abuse. If you are unable to read or process this, you should skip ahead.

Here's the thing, I want to tell you the whole story. I want to tell you the name of my perpetrator, how I knew him (we were related, but that's as much as I can say). I want to say where he is now, and how much it terrifies me that he has children of his own. But I can't. I'll end up in court, and once again, I'll be the defendant. I cannot begin to express how fucked up that is. That you can be sexually abused and raped by someone you know and trust, and because you were five years old and didn't know how to tell anyone, you have to keep it a secret for the rest of your life.

What I can tell you is that early childhood sexual trauma created a blueprint in my psyche that will forever make me doubt, question and fear intimacy and love. It made me want to numb out because I didn't want to experience that kind of pain ever again. Or life itself for that matter. Because life sometimes involves a five-year-old with semen on her bottom and thighs, and who wants to accept a life like that?

Once I got sober, those hazy memories began to come into focus. I was at a family wedding, where my sister and I were flower girls. My sister was three at the time, and they had us wait in one of the hotel rooms, where they made my sister take a nap. For some reason, one of my teenage relatives was also in the room. There were no adults there. Perhaps the teenager was there to watch us. I don't remember what I was doing. Probably playing imaginary games with dolls, pretending I was a magical princess—being a beautiful and innocent child—just like my own daughters.

I know now that when severe trauma happens, our brains protect us. We don't remember much from before or after. Sometimes it takes years to even remember the during.

When it started coming back to me clearly, with all the weight that such a thing carries, it was because I no longer had the drugs in my system that once worked so perfectly to keep the memories at bay. Now sober, I would be in a hotel room, and the smells would suddenly start triggering very visceral reactions. I would feel like my whole body was in shock, that something terrible had just happened. And it had, but about 20 years before.

Back when I was in that hotel room with my little sister and my relative who we'll call "Derrick" (sorry, guys named Derrick). He was telling me how we were supposed to play together. That this is what cousins/brothers/sisters/friends do. My sister was sleeping, and of course I wanted to play, I was five years old. He started pulling his pants down, but even at five, I knew that wasn't supposed to happen.

"Put it away," I told him, turning my head so I couldn't see his penis. He didn't listen, continuing on about how we were just playing, and that this was how kids played. He pulled his pants down, and I looked over to where Gabby slept, instinctually afraid that she might wake up. Instead, he pushed me down over the bed.

"I'm not going to hurt you," he whispered. "We're just having fun..."

But I knew that this wasn't fun. He pushed my puffy white flower girl dress up near my head and started rubbing his penis against my butt and legs. I could hear him grunting and all I could do was bury my head into the comforter. I looked back and asked him to stop and he shoved my head down again, reassuring me that it was almost over.

As Derrick finished, I could feel something wet hit the back of my legs and my butt. I could feel it dripping down my thighs, between the poofs of my pretty white dress. I stood up and turned around. He already had his dress pants back on.

I don't remember anything else. Like how I must have gotten some toilet paper and cleaned my own legs even though I still asked my mommy to wipe me in the potty. I don't remember the burning shame of embarrassment that something really bad had just occurred or that I was really confused about what it was. I don't remember wondering whether I should tell someone. I don't remember getting scared that I would have to see him again.

We are groomed from birth to be good girls. And good girls don't say no, they don't make trouble. They go into the bathroom and clean up their teenage relative's cum from between their legs, even when they're five years old and this should have never happened in the first place.

My next memory of Derrick was a day when I was at the house of another relative. Derrick was over, and I was playing in a bedroom when he snuck in and shut the door. By this point, I knew what was going to happen. He pulled my panties down and again had me lean over the bed. He began to stroke himself. This time he asked me to come down on to the floor and smell his penis. And then he told me to lick it. I followed orders even as I whimpered, "No." Before I knew what was happening, he shoved his penis into my mouth, forcing me to perform oral sex on him.

No one but Derrick knew what happened that day. No one knows to this day how many times it happened.

There's a difference between having parents who are paying attention to you and parents who are too focused on their own lives. And this is not to put all the blame on my mom and dad. They didn't know. They never knew until I got sober, started remembering the years of abuse I suffered and told them. But I also realized that adults who are really present in their children's lives pay attention to the environments they are in; they protect everyone in the room—both the five-year-old child and the teenager. They make sure that children aren't set up to fail.

As a parent, I have a lot on my plate—working at our family's rehab, Alo House, recording the Recovering from Reality podcast, planning wellness events and retreats. Not to mention spending time with my husband, my family and my friends and all the responsibilities that living in the modern world entails—but I also wake up every morning to consciously parent my children. Staying present to the risks and real decisions that parents make, intentionally or otherwise, every day. Decisions that can forever alter the fate of our children's lives.

My mom, who was also abused as a child, once enrolled us in a self-defense class, but by that time it was too little, too late. I just enrolled Harper, my eldest daughter, who turned six this year, in Brazilian Jiu Jitsu. She'll be a killer by the time she's 13. When Harper turned five, my heart broke all over again. The trauma I thought I had worked through came rushing back. She was so delicate, so completely unaware that anyone would ever want to hurt her that way. I couldn't imagine her in that hotel room. I would light myself on fire to stop anything like that from happening.

I was a little girl who just wanted to play imaginary games with my dolls. I was beautiful and innocent, like all little girls are, and I was only five years old. But here is the hardest part of all of this. It happens all the fucking time. Childhood sexual abuse is a silent epidemic in this country—and across the world. We don't want to look at it, so we pretend it doesn't happen. We don't do enough to stop it. We don't prepare our children to protect themselves.

Just like a traumatized person blocks the memories of their victimization, we as a culture have blocked the reality of childhood sexual abuse. And then we pretend that all the horrible things in the world—from rape to mass shootings to addiction—aren't connected to it. The shame that is born from that abuse affects us all. It's like a ripple effect of darkness through our world. And until we bring it into the light, we will all stay sick.

When I was a teenager, I was forced to go to Derrick's wedding, and though I didn't remember all the details yet of what he did to me, I do remember feeling sick as his wife walked down the aisle. I never told anyone because I didn't have the language to explain what happened. I didn't even understand it. I didn't know what sex was, so I certainly didn't understand what rape was. The messages I received, and the education I failed to receive, set me up for failure.

I prepare my girls. They know what to do if anyone ever touches them, tries to pull down their pants or makes them feel weird at all. They know what to say and who to tell. They know not to keep "bad" secrets. They know they can trust me. I teach them what private parts are and what they're called. They accept that we don't allow sleepovers. And despite all of that, I still know that I can't keep them 100 percent safe.

That's the consequence of this epidemic. Because entire generations have failed to bring sexual abuse into the light, shame has grown in the secrets and become part of the shadow aspect of our society. Our parents were molested, their parents were molested and we ended up being molested. No one is supposed to say anything because, God forbid, we would have to look at our culture and how we got here in the first place.

Because even if it wasn't sexual abuse, show me somewhere were children are revered and protected and cherished. Unfortunately, what we see is war and extreme poverty. We watch as children go to bed hungry right here in Los Angeles, one of the wealthiest cities in the world. Children's spirits are smothered to death in industrial factory-style school systems. Child abuse in all forms is inexcusable, and it is something we should fight like hell to eradicate.

Unfortunately, our society would rather live in sickness and in secrets and pretend that everything is fine.

I grew up pretending and I was almost dead by the time I was 20.

The last time I saw Derrick was at the hospital when someone in our family was dying. A couple of years later, when I got sober, I heard he had two daughters, and all I could think of was my sister and I in the hotel room.

When I called the police, I told them I had to report a sexual assault, and though it fell outside of the statute of limitations, I explained that there were children in my perpetrator's home, and that I was concerned for their welfare. The police came to my home, and I sat down with the two officers for an interview. I told them every detail I have shared here. I told them about the hotel room, the grooming and the forced assault. And one of the police officers looked up at me with a warm smile, and said, "Sometimes that's just how kids play together."

I wanted to scream in his face. But instead, I just nodded like a good girl. I was back to being five years old. Back to laying with my face pressed into the comforter, praying my sister didn't wake up and find out who I was. Back to believing that I wasn't beautiful and innocent, that I was just a dirty girl, causing problems. Back to believing that, somehow, I deserved it, and that no one was going to do anything about it anyway.

And sadly, not much has changed in our society.

I was recently at the chiropractor, and when I told him I believed my tension to be connected to my trauma, he asked what happened to me. I was a little surprised by the question, but I believe that others need to know, and I began to share my story with him. I figured he would be a sympathetic audience. Especially because he had been recommended to me by one of my healers.

He started to shake his head, visibly upset.

"No. I just refuse to believe it," he told me, clearly unaware of how powerful words could be. "I hear so many women sharing stories like that. There can't be that many bad guys in the world. It's impossible."

I tried to be patient with him. "Many of them are sick," I responded.

"No," the chiropractor pressed on. "I think people are having false memories. Maybe they hear a story and they believe it happened to them, too." And that's where my patience ended.

For centuries, women have been denied their truths. They have been driven mad by society's refusal to hear their stories, to honor their pain. This shouldn't be my story. But even more so, it shouldn't be *our* story. Because since I started sharing about my sexual assaults, I have found out how *not* alone I am. And it is heartbreaking. Too many of us have a "Derrick" in our story. The "cousin, brother, sister, friend" who became our perpetrator. The person we still can't name or we'll end up facing them in court. The person we have to continue to see at weddings and funerals, reminded of that time when they took everything good and sacred from us, and it took us decades of work and healing to get it back. If we ever did.

A lot of us never get to do the work and healing.

We end up caught up in the trauma. We can't recover from what we don't understand, and we never find the language to explain what happened. Many people never have a moment of peace from the grind of the working-two-jobs world we live in. They're unable to access the "privilege" of getting therapy or other healing support that should actually be a right.

We never learn how to say the words, "I was five years old and I felt his cum on the back of my legs." And we never get to hear an adult professional, perhaps a healer say, "I'm so sorry, that should have never happened to you."

Which is what made my chiropractor's response so devastating.

We never fully get to the other side of this kind of trauma. We recover, but as I sit here right now writing down these memories, I still get stomach cramps. It's not easy. It's hard work. It's a choice to do this work. It's a decision to be present and be willing to look at the whole big beautiful, ugly, scary, amazing picture. Maybe it isn't for everyone. To find the place where we find compassion for ourselves first, then for others. Where we can accept our part, which because a five-year-old obviously has no "part," are the ways we continue to abuse ourselves and others long after our abusers are gone.

We get to the place where we take back our sovereignty and accept the responsibility for fixing the brokenness. Even if that kind of hurt doesn't make sense in a world we want to believe is also magical and miraculous. But the magic comes in being able to heal from it. The miracle is that we survive. And we can hope that other people have that opportunity, too. Even when they're our perpetrator.

Sometimes, we pretend away our shame because reality is just too fucking hard to bear.

And it's understandable. The deep, dark reaches of our interior world can be terrifying. Instead, it's so much easier to focus on the surface: what we look like, who we are dating, and the pictures we post on Instagram.

Or we can face the memories we have tried so hard to avoid.

Sometimes I wish I didn't have those memories. I find myself wishing my childhood was as sweet and innocent as my own daughters' who don't know what an erect penis looks like. (Oh, to be "normal.") But then again, if this hadn't happened, what would my life look like today? Would I have the same point of view? Would I be so passionate about this work? Would I be able say those two magical healing words "me too" to other women who share such similar stories?

Harper and Dakota only know how to play imaginary games with their dolls and pretend they're princesses. They are beautiful and innocent, and I work every day to keep them that way. Does that mean I can protect them everywhere they go? I know that isn't possible. But here's what I can do, what we can all start doing: tell our truths so that the perpetrators don't get to hide in the dark. Sexual assault shouldn't be everyone's secret that finally gets confessed on a therapist's couch, years later. It shouldn't be the big secret we all keep like some rite of passage we have to endure.

It should be something we all shout from the rooftops, to shake off the shame.

Because once we do, we come out of the dark. We step out and shine the brightest fucking light.

## Chapter Three

# Raised by Wolves

*"Out beyond ideas of wrongdoing
and right-doing there is a field.
I'll meet you there.
When the soul lies down in that grass
the world is too full to talk about."*
—*Rumi*

I think when my mom met my dad, her life took a terrible turn. Not that it was stable before, but all of the drama came bubbling up to the surface. Although I am sure she would count having Gabby and I as her greatest achievement, the fact is, she came to Hollywood with much bigger plans than to be a single mom living in an apartment in the Valley.

And she absolutely deserved more than that.

Everyone does.

So instead of seeing her own dreams realized, she turned her attentions to Gabby and me. We were both physically attractive children, and now, when I look at my own children, I realize what a blessing and a curse that is. Beauty might help you to become more popular, to get attention from boys, to get out of trouble. But it also comes with a certain burden. It means people will always judge you first by your surface appearance. They will see your face before they ever see anything else: your heart, your mind and your soul. Your beauty becomes a commodity—something that other people can buy and sell, until you realize that you are in charge of your own beauty, just like you are in charge of your story. You get to decide how you want to use the tools that you have. You get to cut your own path.

My mom wanted us to be the model/actresses she never got to be. And as a result, we never had a chance to just be children. Not only was I quickly becoming the parent in the house, I was also expected to be the source of income. We were no Lindsay Lohan level child-stars, but my mom became her own low-rent version of Dina Lohan, trying to connect us with anyone who might make us famous.

Maybe that's why I still love taking pictures to this day. And though my daughters are in some of those photos, it is their choice to participate. They get to choose how I use their images. Even now, I offer them the opportunity to give consent, to say yes or no. They have the right to determine how their bodies are portrayed, their identities and their roles in this world.

Because that's how we build empowered women. Women who know they have every right to carve their own paths. That right was never extended to me. My mom believed dance classes and modeling shoots would make up for what the men in her life failed to do.

Gabby and I quickly realized we had to find other women to help play the role of mom. When my dad remarried, a strange thing occurred. We fell in love with his new wife. Amy became a source of comfort in our lives. She was young and beautiful and fun. She was loving and nurturing with us, too. Unfortunately, she had no idea what she was in for with my dad.

My mom and Amy would eventually become good friends, which didn't thrill my dad. But Amy was our safe space. She picked us up from school on time and bought us school supplies. She made macaroni and cheese and treated us like kids. She was our constant, and still is. Amy is one of my best friends to this day. She was like a mother and a sister and a friend all at once. I still call her "Amy Mom" or often just "Mom." So when, five years after they were married, my dad told us that they were splitting up, it was like we were being gutted again. She held on for as long as she could, until she couldn't anymore. Without Amy, my dad's drinking only got worse, and since I was older, I could see it.

Alcoholism is a funny thing because most people drink. It's easy to point fingers when people are putting needles in their arms, but what's so wrong about a glass of wine or two or three at dinner? In this way, people can disguise their using as normal, if not downright American. But when you're 10 years old, you can see, smell and *feel* the difference between a beer at dinner and a drunk dad. And you know which one isn't right.

I now have a very different relationship with my dad, and he's proven to be a great grandpa to my girls, but none of that can erase the past. We can forgive, but that doesn't mean we can forget how other people's behaviors influenced our fates, how their choices shaped our own. Until we can all own the truth, we will never be able to fully heal the relationship. He tries hard, sometimes too hard, but we've never quite had that breakthrough in our relationship.

When Gabby and I were with my dad, my job was to monitor his drinking. I would quickly become the adult child of an alcoholic, watching his every move.

"Daddy," I would warn him after we finished dinner at our favorite sushi restaurant. "Are you sure you can drive home?"

I already understood that drinking a bottle of sake and a night's worth of Sapporo was enough to make driving illegal. And I knew that the look in his eyes and the slur in his voice made him unsafe. I would watch the white line, terrified every time he veered over it, checking to see how close we were to the car next to us. I would suck in my breath when he would start yelling at other drivers, honking aggressively as he ripped across the Valley, Gabby and I slamming into each other with every turn. I was just as terrified to say something, but I knew it was my job.

I might not have had anyone to protect me, but Gabby had me.

So I wasn't going to let her down.

One time when this happened, I pulled out my flip phone and started to call my mom. I tried to be as quiet as possible so he wouldn't get mad at me. But then she couldn't hear me over the exhaust of his car with the windows down.

I finally began to yell, crying out to my mom, "Help me!" My dad turned around, swerving his car down Kanan Road. He grabbed my phone, slapping me across the face, before he chucked my phone out the window. I don't know what felt worse, the slap on the face or knowing that I had no ability to call for help.

Imagine you have two beautiful daughters and every time you drink, you terrify them. You know you shouldn't be driving drunk with them. You know you shouldn't hit them. You know you should be a good dad, a loving dad, and yet you can't stop doing the *one* thing that stops you from being that person. You can't quit and so you can't show up. Imagine that guilt. Imagine that pain. It's heartbreaking.

Anger is often just guilt turned inside out. You can't feel bad because then you would have to stop. Instead, you just get angry. Angry at yourself, then angry at everyone else for making you feel guilty. The cycle repeats and the only thing that will stop it is another drink, even as your daughter cries in the back seat. Even as you slap her across the face.

When I got home, my mom just tried to brush it off, which is how my mom handled anything that in got in the way of her plans. At least that is how it felt to me at the time. Because for her, the upside of their divorce was that she now had some weekends off. She could have a break. She could go out on dates or smoke a joint in peace. I get it. It's hard work being a parent. Now when I hear about divorced couples, the one thing I envy them for is having that alone time. Imagine that, a weekend alone? But Gabby and I were tortured and neglected for her freedom.

As much as I would beg not to go to my dad's, we all had our roles in the family. I was the sensitive child. The hypochondriac. The attention seeker. The one not to be trusted. The girl who always cried wolf, despite the fact that all my cries were real. The abuse from my dad continued until I was 13 years old when I came home with a red face and a bruised eye.

"Who did this?" my mom demanded, as though I hadn't been telling her for years about my dad's violence when he drank. I started to cry, suddenly unable to say my dad's name.

"Was it your dad?" she started to yell. I couldn't tell if she was more annoyed about the violence or the fact that she was about to lose her alone time.

But I didn't know what else to say but the truth. I nodded my head and said, "It was Dad."

"Okay," she calmed down, finally accepting the truth. "You don't have to see him anymore if you don't want to." I called my father and told him that I would no longer be seeing or speaking to him.

I wonder now what that moment was like for her. What it's like to be a parent who has been refusing to listen to their child for years, who has failed to protect him or her, and who now must accept that they have been telling the truth all along. My mom wanted the best for me, she loved me with a mother's love, she didn't want me to be hurt and abused. But like my dad, she was a lone wolf—a loving wolf. She wanted to love me, and yet, she wanted her life too. She refused to accept any truth that didn't fit into the picture she had of us.

It took another decade—and a lot more shit—for her to finally step into the truth.

The truth can feel like dogshit at first. It stinks and it's messy, and when you've been working your whole life to avoid it, it can feel like a curse. It feels like the opposite of fate and fairies. It feels hard and unfair. My family didn't want to face that. *I* didn't want to face that, to see the truth for what it was—the path to my divine purpose. Because each injury was actually just the lesson for someone's healing, starting with my own.

The problem with being a parent to yourself, let alone to your biological parents, is that you never get to be a child.

I felt like I was responsible for everyone and their emotions—my father's drinking, my mother's freedom, my sister's safety. And none of them wanted my help. My mom wanted everything on her terms; my dad was the same. My little sister believed I was the problem. She thought that I should shut up and stay in line, that my dad hitting me must have somehow been my fault. People are always so surprised that I am only 28. They think I must be so much older. But the thing is, I've been an adult since I was a kid, so it kind of makes sense.

Around the same time that my father and I stopped talking, his addiction got so bad that nobody wanted to work with him anymore. He became homeless. For 10 years, I barely saw him at all. Then, my mom got remarried. She had a lot of boyfriends by that time—like I said, men who we believed were going to become our new fathers. She started to understand how hard it was for us to get close to these men, so she decided to keep her new romance a secret, finally bringing us to Thanksgiving at his home to introduce us. Though they had been together for six months, it was only the first time we met Jerry.

I was weary and wary by that point but Gabby was much less jaded. She was a lover. She loved everyone and I hated everyone. Maybe if had I gotten to know Jerry better in the beginning, things would have started differently. But only weeks later, my mom and her new boyfriend picked me up from a slumber party with the announcement, "We're getting married!"

What. The. Fuck.

It had been my mom, Gabby and me for years. Now overnight, this new guy was part of our lives. Unfairly, my mom led Jerry to believe that he wouldn't have to take care of us at all financially. She told him that my dad paid child support. Jerry believed that he and my mom would combine their incomes— my mom's income being her alimony and child support—and live a very financially abundant life together. He had no idea my dad was crashing and burning at the time, and that he would soon be living in our garage because he had nowhere else to go.

Jerry wasn't just marrying some my mom, he was marrying her whole crazy family.

Family is a funny thing. We have no choice in the matter. We don't choose to love them, we just do. Even when it might be easier if we didn't. But a stepparent can choose to love, a little bit like a spouse. I choose every day to love my husband. And even though we now share precious daughters, we recognize that choice takes work. It takes practice and patience. I don't think my mom knew how to make those choices in her relationships and my dad certainly didn't. So, as children, Gabby and I experienced the fallout of their choices.

My husband, Evan, and I both say we were raised by wolves. Our parents loved us, but they didn't really know how to do the job properly. Our parents could be kind and loving, they could also be vicious and cruel. They never hesitated to put themselves first. Once we had daughters of our own, we truly understood how much they failed us.

I know that is going to be as hard for them to read as is it for me to write.

I also know that today they are all making a living amends through their relationships with our daughters—or trying to.

I think that's the point of grandparents. They can either repeat the pattern of their parenting, or they can choose to do it over and redeem themselves in the process. We all get the chance to do it over if we're willing to take it. Evan and I are doing it over. We are making the choices that our parents were too sick to even understand were choices. We are offering our children the truths they need to understand this world, while offering them options how they want to navigate it. Of course we're going to fuck up. We're all going to have hard days or make the wrong choice. That's also part of parenting.

Evan and I laugh that one day our girls will end up on the therapist's couch, talking about the Bling Ring and Instagram and their crazy recovered addict parents, but we try to be conscious, even in our mistakes.

We try to be more than wolves. We try to be loving humans, having human experiences, walking through this world the best we can and caring for each other along the way.

------------------------------------------------

## Chapter Four

# A Special Kind of Hell

*"The wounded recognize the wounded."*
—*Nora Roberts*

I feel like everyone knows my story. And at the same time, no one really does. They know the juicy part—the voicemail, the mug shot, the Bling Ring. But they don't know all the stuff that brought me there. That's why I started the podcast and sharing about my life. I wanted people to have another perspective on my life, but also to understand that we can all work through our traumas. I wanted those who've been through something similar to know they aren't alone, and that we can be there for and support one another.

One of the saddest parts about childhood sexual abuse, beyond the violations themselves, is that being abused only increases your chances of being further victimized later in life. Women who have experienced childhood sexual abuse are twice as likely to be raped as adults than someone who hasn't had that early trauma.

How fucked up is that?

The thing is, I understand. After being molested as a child, I had no idea what my body was for. I had no feelings of "my body is a temple and I should respect it." Sex equated love and attention, and since I wasn't receiving the love and attention I needed at home, I became super sexualized at an early age. One thing that still baffles me is that, before we were even in sixth grade, my mother allowed us to wear thongs, low-rise jeans and tight, short t-shirts that showed our bare midriffs. Then when I was 17, she even let Tess and I go to Paris *by ourselves* to model lingerie. People in my life contributed to my exploitation in many different ways, either actively or through negligence.

Before you read on, please know that this chapter will contain stories of sexual violence and assault. If you are not comfortable with this material, feel free to skip to the next chapter.

I have stayed silent to protect people my whole life, so I refuse to do that here.

After my dad's third marriage broke up, he began dating a new lady. Ryan was as much of a mess as my dad. Whereas Amy, my now ex-stepmom, was a safe and stable force, Ryan was dangerous and chaotic. She told everyone she was sick, but we quickly figured out it was just a front to get sympathy, money and drugs. Since she spent most her time in bed on heavy narcotics, Gabby and I played in my dad's room. We were little kids and just looking for love and affection. Though we both didn't understand it at the time, what Ryan offered as love and affection was actually sexual abuse.

She would have us play with her big boobs as she lay in bed wearing nothing but a thong. We had no idea there was anything wrong with this. We were just excited that someone was paying attention to us. Because our dad certainly wasn't.

It's so hard to be a parent and not imagine my own daughters in these circumstances. I guess that's why the universe gave me two daughters, just like Gabby and me. I see them and, though my six-year old has started to get more curious about her body, she wouldn't even think to participate in such an act. I grew up believing that these sexual ideas came from me. That I was the bad one. I was the girl with the scarlet letter (if I'd actually read that book in high school). The truth is, I was just a little girl who needed people to take care of me. And instead, I was treated like a little adult, so I became one. I acted like an adult. I mimicked adult behavior. I was sexualized by so many people around me; I thought I was the sexual one. But I wasn't, I was just a child.

It was only a matter of time before someone else took advantage of my trauma.

Ironically, beyond the relative who raped me, it was women who sexually abused me most throughout my childhood. I think a lot of women overlook this fact. It's so easy to identify men as the perpetrators, and that is certainly more often the case, but if a girl or woman does something, that's only playing, right? Because woman-on-woman experiences are so overly sexualized by our culture, people frequently refuse to see them as violent. Instead, many girls grow up carrying the shame of what they've done with other girls and women, not realizing that they were being sexually abused the whole time.

Unfortunately, many women are afraid to tell their stories because they don't want to be exploited further. We deserve a safe space to share what happened to us, and to be able to understand our own victimizations. A lot of women don't understand we were molested because society tells us that X is rape and Y isn't, that A is abuse, but not B. So we live in silence about what happened to us. In being honest, we can finally see our stories in each other's experiences. We can finally say, "Fuck that, I was abused, I was raped, I was molested, I was hurt." We can finally mirror our hurt and our healing. And we should be able to share those truths without worrying how our pain might be exploited for another's pleasure.

I never again want my truth to be used for someone else's arousal, but I'm also not going to be silenced to protect your sickness. We should all have the space to share our truths. That's the space where we begin to heal, and I feel the same for the perpetrator too.

When I was 12 years old, my mom had married Jerry and she wanted to focus on her new marriage. I get it. She had been raising two girls by herself for seven years.

Now, she had a new husband and she was hoping for a second chance at life.

We moved into a nice house, and things were looking better for us than they had in years. We never really went on vacation, so my mom and Jerry decided to take us to the Embassy Suites up in Oxnard. Real exciting, I know. Since they wanted some time alone, they invited an older local girl who we'll call "Heather" to come with us, so she could watch us while they went out to dinner and drank by the pool. Heather lived in my neighborhood and I was friends with her sister. On one of those days, I saw Heather flirting with a boy down by the pool. I thought he was cute. After we went back up to the room, I asked Heather about the boy.

She started egging me on, asking, "Oh, do you like him?"

I was only 12 and still shy about boys, but I admitted I did.

Heather asked me, "Do you want to be cool?"

I'm sure I said yes, because what 12-year-old doesn't want to be cool? Then Heather told me that she could teach me how to kiss. I told her no, kind of freaked out that my babysitter would offer that. But then she started taking off her clothes. She told me that boys liked it when you played with your boobs. I didn't even have boobs, so I had no idea what she was talking about. She forced herself upon me, touching me and putting her finger inside me. I knew what she was doing was wrong, and yet she kept telling me it was normal.

The thing is, I knew that I always liked girls, but this isn't the way that I wanted to be touched. I knew it wasn't consensual. She went on to ask me to record a video of her playing with herself on her phone. I did it. I am just so grateful that she didn't convince me to make a video of myself as well. I assume Heather had been abused herself. Not that it is an excuse. Despite the stereotype, the chain of sexually abused to abuser is not automatic. By the time Heather was 16, she was pregnant. A few short years later, she began her stints in jail and prison. Shortly after Heather's last release, 10 years after she abused me, they found her dead from an OD.

A couple years ago, I took a test for Adverse Childhood Experiences (ACE), which measures the 10 biggest traumatic events that you can go through in your life. Not only does your ACE "score" measure your risk of becoming an addict but it also predicts whether you will suffer from depression or other mental health disorders, including your risk of dying by suicide. It also measures your risk of having cancer, heart disease and obesity. I ended up scoring nine out of 10. I remind myself every day that I am lucky to be alive. Because those early childhood traumas affect every part of our existence—from our mental health to our physical well-being.

Trauma, and stress caused by trauma, are known to be one of the main causes of academic struggle for children and teenagers and are also likely causes of Attention Deficit Disorder (ADD). Looking back, it makes sense that I couldn't comprehend what was happening in school, considering I couldn't understand what was happening outside of it either.

It was like I only had so much room in my head.

In third grade, I had a teacher who kept me after class every day to try to explain things in a way I could understand. Then I would go home, and everything would feel so crazy; it was too hard to hold on to the lesson I had just been given. I was put on Adderall, pure amphetamine salts, when I was 12.

They say that one of the biggest remedies for childhood trauma is having a stable and attuned adult who you can trust and count on, which builds resiliency. But I had so few stable adults, if any, that this wasn't an option. I was lost at sea, and every time I found someone I thought I could trust, I would cling to that person like I was drowning.

When I was 13, I started dating my first boyfriend. He was a nice, sweet boy from a big Italian-American family. I remember feeling so safe at his house. I would walk three miles to go over there after school, and his mother would ask, "Where is your mom? Why couldn't she drive you here?" Vito was probably my last healthy relationship before I met my husband, Evan.

He was kind to me; his family was kind to me. Every family has their own drama, of course, but in his, they stuck together through it all.

Every Sunday, they'd have family dinner together. It was mandatory. His mother would be cooking sauce all day (and still to this day, I've never had a better marinara). But that small taste of normalcy wasn't enough to counteract my life at home. All that old trauma started to surface once I hit adolescence. In many ways, trauma is like a volcano. It simmers below during childhood and then it just erupts, blowing up into bad behaviors and dangerous choices.

I started acting out sexually, trying to figure out who I was. By the time I was 14, I started smoking pot with my mom. By the time I was 15, I was addicted to a number of substances. That trauma ran like lava through my life, burning anything that was good and true in its path. I learned that to score drugs without any money, I had to use the only gift I believed I had been given: my looks. It wasn't that I had to have sex with people. Sometimes I just had to make them think there was a chance I would have sex with them. But it didn't matter. Either way, I began to view myself as something to be bought and sold.

I didn't realize that with every encounter, every violent boyfriend, every blowjob traded for a little bag of dope, I was only re-traumatizing myself. I was disconnecting myself further from the little girl who learned at the age of five that her body wasn't hers, and it would never be. The shame became so deep that it didn't feel like I had any choice but to embrace it, to believe that abuse was power.

I didn't understand the purpose of my body. It was just this thing that had been used and abused, that I then used and abused. I tried to kill it. And I allowed other people to do the same. It wasn't until I got pregnant with Harper that I began to see my body as a beautiful force. I started to see it as something to be revered, to be treated with love and respect. I now recognize my body is a powerful vessel, one that I can honor or desecrate through my choices.

But back then, I didn't know how to love myself. I only knew how to escape myself. And I was just getting started.

## Chapter Five

# Learning to Escape

*"It isn't the drug that causes the harmful behavior — it's the environment. An isolated rat will almost always become a junkie. A rat with a good life almost never will, no matter how many drugs you make available to him... Addiction isn't a disease. Addiction is an adaptation. It's not you — it's the cage you live in."*
*—Johann Hari, Chasing the Scream*

When you're a teenager who has never been taught a single coping skill, there is only one way through pain, and that is escape. I learned early how to escape — television and boys — but perhaps my biggest distraction was Tess. Though we were both each other's greatest friends, we were also really dangerous together. I'm not blaming her; there was something about the way we mixed that brought out the worst in me. There was something dangerous and chaotic about our relationship. I was recently telling Tess this, but she had no idea what I was talking about.

I don't want to tell Tess' story because it's hers to share, but I will say this, next to Tess' family life, mine looked kind of normal. As unstable as our family was, my mom's house felt safer. Tess and I had been through a lot of the same things, and those pains created their own trauma bond between us. We were like magnets to each other, and whether we were best friends or in the middle of a huge fight, I was obsessed with our relationship. Even now, so many years later, I realize there are areas where I need to detach, but our bond is so deep, it's hard to let go.

Tess and I had both suffered from our own forms of abuse, and since we weren't able to act out our emotions on our perpetrators, instead we did it to each other. We pushed each other into bad behaviors, always trying to prove ourselves, no matter how high the stakes. And since the last thing I wanted to do was to focus on me, I focused on us. We would see the other kids doing well in school, going home to what we assumed were happy homes, acting like normal kids, whose parents didn't get drunk and hit them, and it only solidified our bond. It was us against them, like blood sisters who kept cutting each other to prove our friendship.

I loved Tess so much, no matter how much I felt bullied by her. I remember being in fifth grade and we were hanging out with a group that included a boy I liked. We were all laying on his bed reading comic books, when Tess pulled down my shirt in front of everyone. She exposed my breasts and embarrassed me in front of the boy and our other friends. But I didn't know how to stand up to her. She was the only person who understood where I came from. She was the only person I thought I could trust.

By the time we made it to high school, my mom saw an opportunity for Tess and me to become models. Finally, we were old enough for her to begin to capitalize off of what she had recognized since we were little girls: people paid attention to us. My mom enrolled us both in modeling classes and we started working. But then Tess' dad found out that my Mom took us down to Alvarado Street in LA to get fake IDs and he rightfully freaked out. Tess' dad had his own history with drugs and alcohol, but he was clean and desperately trying to help his daughter. This was around the same time when Tess and I started fighting more. And I can only imagine my Mom's frustration. It was like parenting teenage sisters, except we weren't actually sisters. Tess's dad wanted her home, and I wanted her out.

Like any drug, as soon as she was gone, I was lost. She was the sun in my solar system and now I had to go out and find new friends on my own. My mom and I were living in Agoura Hills, and I had just started high school. At this point, I stopped all extra-curricular activities because of a really bad foot injury that I got in dance class. Now, I was stuck on crutches after a brutal surgery. There an upside though: the broken foot came with a Vicodin prescription.

I had gotten drunk before so it wasn't my first high, but that Vicodin did something to me that nothing else had. With it, I felt both alive and dead. It was like all the pain that I had lived in my whole life was magically removed. Vicodin was the perfect escape. For the first time in my life, I actually felt happy. I tried to return to school after my procedure, but shortly after, I stopped going altogether. My mom got tired of being harassed by the school administration, so she pulled me out and started "homeschooling" me instead, which really just meant that I got to sit around all day and smoke pot and take Vicodin. I was 14, and within a matter of months, I became a dropout and a drug addict.

I was too fucked up to care about any consequences. It wasn't until I got sober that I realized that someone *should* have been caring about those consequences for me. For so long, I had been parenting myself, Gabby and even Tess and no one was parenting me. I had no idea.

Vicodin became the closest thing to safe I had felt in a long time. I could lie in bed and fade away. And it felt like no one could touch me there. Now, when I look at pictures of myself from that time, it's heartbreaking. Because in many ways, we're all still kids at 14. So young and naïve and awkwardly opening up to what the future might hold. But you can see that the light is already dimming in my eyes.

At 15, I was losing hope. Then Tess came back. She had a long history of running away. Sometimes she would end up at her boyfriend's house, and other times, at ours. This time, she moved back in, and things began to feel normal. I was dating a new guy, Kevin. Kevin wasn't a bad kid, but he was already doing bad things—using and selling drugs. Tess and I started partying with him. We brought Gabby along for the ride—literally. The thing was, Gabby was the one who always tried to have a normal life. When we were being homeschooled—I mean smoking pot— Gabby actually tried to continue to go to school.

One night, Tess and Gabby went out with Kevin. They came to pick me up later in the day. As we were driving around, a piece of foil appeared. I watched Tess light it up from underneath. She then inhaled the burning smoke from a small glass pipe.

A part of me hesitated but I asked, "Is that coke?"

Kevin laughed, "This shit is so much better than coke."

Tess exhaled the smoke and told me, "It's Oxy."

I didn't know what Oxy was, but Tess and Kevin were doing it. I was so obsessed with being cool; the last thing I was going to do was look like a loser in front of my best friend and boyfriend. I swallowed that dark feeling deep into the pit where I kept all the emotions I refused to feel. I shrugged my shoulders like I could care less, and when they asked if I wanted any, I replied, "Sure, why not?"

I inhaled the crackling pill, breathing the burning chemical in deep. I felt that same sense of safety that Vicodin had offered me, but times a million. Oxy didn't just make me feel safe; it made me feel like I was in Fort Knox. If Fort Knox was made of clouds and cotton candy. I was enveloped with love and comfort. I was feeling everything I imagine my children must feel when they lay in their parents' bed, wrapped up in our arms, believing that as long as Mommy and Daddy are there, nothing can ever hurt them. By the time the high began to fade, the pipe was back in front of me. Just in time to send me back to safety, to the place I had been searching for my whole life.

For years, Tess and I had been entrenched in each other's secrets. Since we were children, we were the only safe space for each other. But as we got older, that secret space was becoming increasingly dangerous. We used to be each other's escape, but now we were escaping together. We kept pushing each other into worse behavior.

In our family system, we had all taken on our roles: I was the scapegoat, Gabby was the forgotten child and Tess was the troublemaker. I went where Tess went, and Gabby followed us both. Unfortunately, I also took the blame. I think I became hard-wired to take responsibility because it felt like no one else around me would. Everyone else shrugged off their roles and duties. They blamed someone else or they lived in denial. When shit hit the fan, everyone else ran, while I found myself holding the bag. Later, that bag would be a literal bag. But I don't want to get ahead of myself. The hard truth was, Tess and I were just two scared little girls who thought if we pretended we were tough, maybe we wouldn't get hurt anymore. Once we started smoking Oxys, we had a new mission in life: get more.

The worst people on the planet (next to pedophiles) are guys who will give dope to teenage girls.

My mom didn't seem to notice our newfound passion for getting and using Oxy. The thing is, now that Tess was back, my mom was once again focused on making us stars. The Kardashians had just come out with their TV show, and since we lived Calabasas adjacent, my mom figured we could be doing the same thing. She started representing us, trying to book us on modeling gigs. She had us take pole dancing classes, and before you knew it, we were posing topless in front of weird photographers we met on the website Model Mayhem. My mom would excitedly send us off to each shoot, hoping it was going to be our big break.

It didn't seem to matter that Tess and I were getting fucked up the whole time. My mom was convinced that she could finally turn our double trouble into a paycheck, and that was what was important. Then we actually started booking gigs. And it looked like finally, after years of trying, my mom's dreams of stardom might really come true. There's probably no greater escape than fame. You don't even have to focus on your reality if you're recreating it every day. You can lose yourself entirely to what other people think of you, what they say about you. You can ignore all the pain and trauma and focus instead on what *may* be. Because the next big thing is always coming. My mom was convinced the big break was on its way for all us. She was manifesting it.

I got my GED and was finally done with school. I thought I would never go back. All I thought I needed was my headshot, my street smarts and my opioids— I would be fine. The brushes with fame began to grow like wildfire and Tess and I were the fuel. We thought for sure we would make it, which was great, because we needed money for our deepening drug habit. We had to keep up our great escape even as life was finally taking off.

------------------------------------------------------

## Chapter Six

# Living the Lie

*"People will do anything, no matter how absurd,*
*in order to avoid facing their own souls.*
*One does not become enlightened by imagining figures of*
*light, but by making the darkness conscious."*
—*Carl Jung*

Tess and I sat in the car parked outside the studio. I was a little nervous, but Tess looked like she was about to jump out the window with excitement. I pulled out the eight ball of coke that I stole from my boyfriend, and we quickly snorted a couple of lines. Tess's shoulders moved up and down with her eyebrows, the coke amplifying an already thrilling moment.

"Marilyn Fucking Manson," she hissed with a smile.

"Marilyn Fucking Manson," I replied, slipping the baggie back into my bag, which also carried a bottle of Oxys and a pint of vodka. We had been booked for a Marilyn Manson video shoot, and we came to party. The next eight hours were a blur. We basically walked into the shoot, got rid of our clothes, and partied in our lingerie while Manson and his band performed and the production crew shot whatever video was actually being filmed.

Tess and I didn't care. We were having too much fun with the guys—doing lines and shots of vodka, running off to the bathroom to snort our pills because we didn't have enough to share.

At 5am, we emerged. We rushed back to our car, wrapped in the blankets the production crew had given us, as excited as we were walking in. We drove to an IHOP and got breakfast. We had found the greatest job on the planet: getting paid to party like rock stars, with rock stars. I sat back in the booth, barely able to eat the pancakes I ordered, smiled and said, "This is the fucking good life."

For much of the late 2000s, Tess and I weren't poor teenagers from the Valley thrown together through trauma and bad parenting, we were 20-year-old socialites who were trying to make it in the shadow of the celebrity kids who came before us—Paris and Nicky, Nicole Richie and those Kardashian girls. My mom quickly realized that our modeling options would be limited if we used our real ages. But the façade was about more than just how old we were. We would go to clubs and be let in without any questions.

We were the life of the party, so promoters wanted us there. No one was going to card the life of the party.

Talk about escape. I was not only getting to escape from my emotions, but from my entire identity. I was able to leave that old Alexis behind and become a new and improved version. And people loved it. Tess and I exuded something we never really had as kids—confidence. We weren't the poor kids in the rich neighborhood anymore. We were the stars. While being a star means you get to shine really bright for a moment, you're destined to burn out. Even though we had just gotten started, the light was already beginning to flicker.

But how could we stop partying when we were the party? Coke, Oxy, heroin, booze, whatever pills we could get our hands on. We were beautiful trashcans, consuming everything in our wake, eventually passing out next to each other, or next to whoever supplied us with drugs the night before. We weren't sure where we were going, but we were determined, we were stars.

I'm not even sure we knew what that meant; my mom was driving the whole endeavor. The truth was, all Tess and I really wanted to be was high. But that night in the parking lot, about to shoot a music video with Marilyn Fucking Manson, being 16 and loaded on booze and coke and Oxy, partying with one of the biggest celebrities in the world at the time, we were on top of the world.

That was just the beginning. Not long after that, Tess met a rock star and hooked up with him all summer. Though Tess was 19 and I was 18, everyone thought we were in our early 20s. We looked it, we acted it and that became the story we sold. We were no longer hanging on the fringes of fame. We were right in the middle of it. We went to parties at this rock star's house, who we'll call "John" in Malibu with all these crazy famous people—Cindy Crawford, members of The Red Hot Chili Peppers and more. One night, John took us out to dinner at a little Italian restaurant in Malibu, where Sean Penn joined us.

Afterward, on our way home, Tess asked me, "Oh my God, can you believe Sean Penn was flirting with you?"

"Who?" I asked, having no clue who she was talking about.

She laughed at me. "Um, *Fast Times at Ridgemont High*?"

Ah, yes.

A couple of nights later, we were partying at John's, when someone made the decision that we would all go over to Sean's place. It was a particularly wild night. I'll never forget the image of Sean Penn putting on my favorite bright red lipstick—which is to this day, Dior 999—and doing a crazy monologue. Sean and I hit it off. He kissed me goodnight and we exchanged numbers, texting all the way up until I was arrested in October. When the police confiscated my phone, I remember telling the officer, "Um, I'm going to need that back, I'm texting with Sean Penn."

I remember being blown away by everyone's talent and creativity. I felt like a fraud, but the truth was,

I was just 20 to 30 years younger than most of them. No one knew how young we were. We didn't look like teenagers.

After Sean completed his crazy monologue, I leaned over to Tess and whispered, "I think I'm more fucked up than anyone here."

Tess nodded dully, slurring her reply, "Meee too…"

Years later, I had a counselor who told me, "You know most people would never even try heroin, right?" I was shocked to hear this. But even during those years, I was beginning to get the sense that the way Tess and I partied was different. It wasn't just the drugs we did (which eventually included heroin); it was the way we did them. Other people could go home and sleep it off, but Tess and I always needed more, more, more. We needed drugs to function, to feel, to connect, to participate in life. They say that addiction is fun at first, and then fun with problems and then just problems. We were in the fun phase, and yet there was something about it that still felt desperate.

Another night we were at John's place with a bunch of other celebrities. John was playing some of his new music on the guitar when I realized I was out of heroin. The last thing I wanted to do was start crashing in front of Cindy Crawford. Tess didn't have any drugs either, which was no surprise. I was the mule for most of our friendship. If Tess had her own stash, it was usually gone before mine.

"I'm gonna go re-up," I told her.

"Sweet," Tess replied. She never had any money either, so when we ran out, it was my job to get more. Thankfully, we had just been paid for the Marilyn Manson gig.

That night leaving the party, I didn't even think twice about driving high down PCH, I just did it. I drove everywhere, every day, high as could be. I was an 18-year old junkie. Concern for my own life was void; and my concern for others barely showed up on the radar.

That's one of the saddest parts about addiction. It wasn't just that I didn't care about myself, though that was horribly tragic. I simply didn't give a shit about anyone. I didn't even see that anyone else was there. I was so caught up in my own needs, my own escape, that I couldn't see where anyone else was walking, let alone walk in their shoes. Children grow up with child-mind—they can only view the world as though they are at the center of its solar system. And when you never get the chance to mature properly, you get stuck in that thinking. I was the center of the solar system, and the only thing I could think about was how to get high.

That night, I drove through the winding, dark roads of Malibu Canyon and into the Valley, nearly crashing because the fog was so thick. I was sitting in the car off of Laurel Canyon, waiting for my dealer to meet me. The window was rolled down a couple of inches as I smoked a cigarette, feeling the excitement that always came on right before the dealer arrived. It was like I was already getting high, my mouth filling with saliva, knowing that relief was near. I didn't hear anyone approach the car, music blasting, oblivious to anything but my phone as I waited for it to ring.

"Get the fuck out of the car!" were the first words I heard.

I didn't see who said them, but there was a gun pointed just inches from my head, caught in the crack of my rolled down window.

All I could think was, "I need to get the fuck out of here," as I shifted into drive and hit the gas as hard as I could.

As I drove off, I heard the guy screaming behind me, "My gun, my gun!" I realized that the gun was still stuck in my driver side window. I pushed it out with my elbow. Even in my fucked up state, I was careful not to touch it.

All I knew was that I needed to get out of there. Fast.

I drove and drove, sobbing hysterically, finally stopping on Ventura Blvd, when I was sure that no one was following me. I called Tess crying.

"What's wrong, Alexis? What's wrong?" Tess asked as I cried over the phone. She put me on speaker phone as I told her and John the story.

"Don't worry," he told me. "We'll come get you." This massive rock star was offering to come rescue me, but I was more concerned about getting high.

"No, I'll be fine," I told him. "I'm just going to go home." I hung up and called my dealer, telling him what happened. It didn't even occur to me that he might have told my would-be robber where I would be waiting for him. He showed up minutes later to the new location. As soon as he left, I heated up the H on some foil and got high in the front seat of my car on Ventura, as cars whipped past me, waiting for my calm to return.

I wish I could say that was the end, but it was only the beginning. I had just turned 18, and it felt like the problems were already consuming the fun. Some people can go on using for decades. The problems build slowly. They're not overwhelmed by their choices, or maybe their consequences just aren't that heavy. But I felt like I was already dealing with life or death problems. I would wake up in one bad situation or another, and I would wonder, "What am I doing wrong?" Any normal person would have shouted, "Drugs, stupid!" I couldn't see that the Oxy, heroin, coke or weed was a problem. I just thought it was what I was using to survive. And I had been trying to survive all my life.

One night, I spent the night with a drug dealer friend of mine. When his girlfriend came home the next morning and found me in his bed, she beat the shit out of me. The following year, I was out partying in LA with a new group of friends; some guys were top financial bulldogs, others were club promoters. We were having dinner at one of their hotspots and one of the guys, who we'll call Bryan, invited us back to his house.

When we got to his house, I suddenly felt very intoxicated. I found a bedroom with an adjoining bath and turned on the shower. I sat down in my clothes underneath the overhead faucet. Instead of sobering up, I began to feel even more fucked up. When I came to, I was in Bryan's bed and he was on top of me. I felt like I was suffocating.

I don't remember much, but the next thing I knew, he was forcing his penis into my mouth. I was trying to get away but I couldn't move. I felt like I was made of Jell-O. Then he turned me around and pushed himself inside me.

I remember saying, "No, no! I don't want to do this." How do you fight back when you know there's no way you'll win? Most girls my age were figuring out what they were going to wear to prom and debating what colleges they were going to apply to, I was an 18-year old junkie getting raped.

The next time I came to, it was around five in the morning. Tess had left with one of the other guys, leaving me alone in Bryan's house. I called a cab and got out of there, pretending nothing out of the ordinary had happened. I had given up being normal so many years before; I just shrugged it off.

Getting raped was the price of being an addict.

This is the fate for a lot of female addicts. When you sit in the rooms of AA, you hear the stories over and over. Childhood sexual abuse, rape, sexual assault—intimate violations are practically a prerequisite for substance use disorders. We don't even question it. We are in so many unsafe circumstances with dangerous people, our abilities and inhibitions low; we don't even believe ourselves when we say no. Instead, we just think this is something we deserve. Because chances are, if we're battling substance abuse, we're probably already coming from a place of diminished or non-existent self-esteem. People don't trust us, and we don't trust ourselves.

The thing was, I was still hoping someone might show up to protect me. I desperately wanted just one person who I could trust, and who believed I deserved more than the life I was living. And later that year, I started casually dating that someone. Neal Brennan was one of the hottest comedians in town in 2009. He was Dave Chappelle's writing partner on *The Chappelle Show*, and he seemed like a real grown up.

We met one night at a party and talked until the sun came up.

He was a smart, normal, nice guy and he thought I was 21. I was totally in love with him. He embodied everything I wanted to be. I think he cared about me too, until he realized that the smart, funny girl he met at the club was also seriously fucked up. One night, he asked me out to dinner. I asked him to pick me up from Beso, a regular hot spot where Tess and I would drink. We left Tess at the bar as Neal and I went out to get Ethiopian food. I was not a fan of the food but I was a fan of Neal's. I thought the date was going great, until Neal got a call from the manager at Beso. Apparently, Tess rang up a sizable tab in his name at the bar while we were gone.

We were both horrified. After he cleaned up the mess, we went back to his place, but I could tell that something was wrong. I smoked heroin in his bathroom and passed out in bed next to him. The next morning, he woke me up. Adding to my total embarrassment that morning, I needed to ask him for a ride all the way home. Cringe worthy, I know. Tess took my car and said she went to Vegas that night, though it would turn out she was really at Nick Prugo's house.

I was stuck in LA, and Neal wanted me gone.

"Come on," he said. "I'll take you home." I didn't even argue with him. I knew the gig was up. Like most people, Neal believed I was a socialite just hanging out in the Hollywood scene, but as he drove me to Agoura Hills in his little Prius, he began to see the holes in my story.

"I thought you were from Holmby Hills," he said, mentioning the exclusive enclave Tess and I used to pretend was home—the same neighborhood where Michael Jackson died the following year.

"No. West Hills," I told him, as though he must have just heard wrong. Over the course of the next hour in the car, Neal told me I was a beautiful, smart, lovely girl and that I was destroying my life.

Finally, he asked the question I had been asking myself a lot lately: "What the fuck is wrong with you?"

I had been staring out the window the whole time, cool-eyed and calm, but finally, my age betrayed me. Tears filled my eyes, as I looked down and replied, "I don't know."

Finally, we arrived at my parents' house. Neal nodded his head quietly, the kind of nod that says goodbye without having to say it.

"Be careful, out there," he finally offered. "Okay, Alexis?" I grabbed my bag and rushed into my house without even saying goodbye. I still feel the pain of that moment to this day. I was heart-broken and ashamed, but I had no space for these emotions.

Active addiction doesn't allow you to feel real emotion. Sadness hits, but the addict brain refuses to experience it. It gets buried it deep under the immediate needs—getting drugs, getting high, getting the escape. I couldn't go home and let myself cry and feel. I couldn't walk through anything hard. I had a fast pass out of pain, and I was desperate to use it before I was caught in the vicious spin of everything I had ever refused to feel. If I dropped in too deep, I might never get out.

Instead, I could only call my dealer.

I didn't know how to feel bad for what had happened, or to hear the words that Neal was saying. I knew he meant them from a good place, and even worse, I knew that they were true. But I also knew that I had no intention of being careful. I was careless in everything I did: who I hung out with, who I slept with, what drugs I did and with who. I was careless with my body and other people's emotions. I was careless with my sweet, sacred soul. I didn't see myself as anything unique or divine. I didn't see that there was a world around me with its own needs and issues. I didn't see other people's pain or concern. I was selfish and self-absorbed; I hadn't been taught to be any other way.

## Chapter Seven

# The Age of Reality

*"We have to dare to be ourselves, however frightening or strange that self may prove to be."*
—May Sarton

At this point, Tess and I were living double lives. We would go to auditions—getting parts in music videos and small movies—then later that same day, we would be out on the streets, panhandling for drugs. One minute we would be in the VIP section at the Mondrian, and two hours later, we would be cruising through Skid Row trying to score. Tess was now 19, which made everything feel a little more legitimate, even though I was still 18. My mom knew something was wrong with us, but we kept ending up in the right place at the right time. What was she going to say?

That I had a curfew? That I couldn't do drugs in the house? That I was a teenager and had to listen to my mother? Hardly. I had been running the house since the age of 10. I had been the adult for so long, she couldn't all of a sudden come in and act like she was the parent and I was the child. And now I was both making the money and making things happen. Tess and I would walk into a club and the club would slow down. No one knew who we really were, but everyone loved us. And we were starting to get more work.

We landed a small part in a movie called *Frat Party*, and figured Lindsay Lohan-level success was right around the corner. Once again, we became known as much for our antics as our talent. Everyone on set thought we were out of control, but it was a car wreck they enjoyed watching. One of the actors on the movie, a comedian named Dan Levy, thought we were hysterical—these two wild party girls growing up in LA with a new age-y mother who was a former *Playboy* playmate.

Around the same time, Tess, herself became a playmate. She was 18 and Hugh Hefner's TV show, *The Girls Next Door*, was a huge hit. Tess was determined to be cast on the show and be one of Hugh's girlfriends, which sounded as disgusting to me then as it does now. I didn't agree with her life goal, but when Dan proposed that we shoot a sizzle reel for a reality show, we both saw it as a great opportunity. Maybe Tess' dream was to become Hugh Hefner's girlfriend; mine was to never have to worry about running out of drugs again.

Reality TV was just becoming a big thing, and my mom was stoked. Finally, we were getting the shot at fame she had been seeking our whole lives. She had recently read *The Secret*, which actually came out of a philosophical tradition called the "New Thought Movement" that she'd studied for much of her life. At a young age, my mom was introduced to a book called *Science of Mind* by a man named Ernest Holmes. Holmes and others believed that humans are able to participate in the creation of reality, much more so than we currently realize.

Of course, given the age we live in, this turned into something much more crass: manifesting abundance, where abundance simply means money. My mom was obsessed with vision boards and affirmations and chanting for success. She would have us sit around and hold hands, praying for the reality show, as though that was one of the gifts the Universe grants on the regular. My mom believed that we had a message to share, and that fame would give us an avenue for that message.

I now understand what she meant. It's just that I didn't really have a message at that point. I didn't have anything worthwhile to say or to offer. And fame on its own is just an empty stage. Now I understand that fame isn't the end. It's the means. It's the way to connect to people and share experience and hope. But back then, I didn't understand my experience, and I didn't have any hope to give.

We shot the sizzle reel for the show, and Dan captured all of it on tape: my mom chanting for fame,

Tess and I partying in the clubs, the auditions and wild nights. Though it was clear that there was no actual homeschooling going on, unless vision boarding was a class, Dan thought it was all insane and amazing. We didn't know if anything would happen with it, but when Dan called us and told us that there was a bidding war between A&E and E!, we were beside ourselves.

My mom screamed, "The chanting worked! The chanting worked!"

The next year, I became famous for something much bigger than the reality show, so obviously the affirmations weren't a perfect science. Both E! and A&E wanted the show. A&E was at the height of *John and Kate Plus Eight* fame, but E! had something else. Not only were the Kardashians already proving to be a winning template for the network, but late night talk show host, Chelsea Handler, wanted to produce our show.

We couldn't believe this was happening to us.

"I'm definitely going to get noticed by *Playboy* now!" Tess shrieked, delighted.

All I could do was wait for the check to arrive after the pilot was officially picked up. I didn't really understand why we were doing the show, but I did know that being famous meant free shit—free booze, free drugs, free clothes—a welcome relief after growing up with such a sense of scarcity and financial fear. For so long, our lives had been about what we didn't have—we didn't have a dad, we didn't have enough money, we didn't have peace in our home, we didn't have what we wanted—and everyone seemed to be miserable. Now, it looked like that lack might finally be changing. We would have money and with that, we assumed, happiness. I later found out money can buy comfort, but it offers little guarantee of happiness.

It was around this time that we started hanging out more with Tess' friend from one of the alternative high schools she attended. Nick Prugo was a young gay kid who liked to party like we did. He lived at home with his parents but told everyone he was a stylist. He adored Tess and would give us clothes to use for photo shoots. She would use him to hook us up with clothes and drugs. And he always seemed to have cash on him, or at least a lot more than us.

We found out later that most of the clothes he gave us were stolen. A lot of our friends had big wardrobes—we had no reason to think that Nick was taking items from Rachel Bilson's closet. Plus, we were party girls getting free stuff. We really weren't going to go *Law & Order: SVU* on Nick's clothing hookup. It seemed to work for him, and so it worked for us, too.

When you're using drugs, you learn not to ask questions. The mafia calls it "omerta" and it's the code of silence between thieves. When you're an addict, omerta applies to yourself, too. You don't even ask yourself too many questions. You go through life without asking yourself why you do the things you do. You certainly don't question the person smoking Oxys or shooting up next to you. You just stay quiet, get high and try to make it through the day to score again. Part of getting sober is beginning to ask questions—first of ourselves, then of our friends and family. Ultimately, we start to get outside ourselves enough to start asking questions of the world and the universe. But back then, all I could do was get by.

Tess started missing photo shoots and not making it to auditions. She would go out with whoever her boyfriend was at the time and disappear for days. My mom was getting pissed. It's easy to classify her as a stage mom, but she saw it as a real opportunity for all of us. She had been struggling her whole life, and finally Tess and I were giving her a clear path out of that struggle. The last thing she wanted was for us to fuck it up. So finally, my mom had enough. She told Tess to shape up or get out. Tess wasn't anywhere near shaping up, so she left our house and moved in with Nick instead.

Though the show had been picked up, we still had a few months before we would begin shooting. Gabby and I were still living at home with my mom. Gabby was back in a real high school, but she was now doing modeling and music videos as well. My mom would try to package her alongside Tess and I, and once Tess moved out, in place of her. Though Gabby had done her fair share of partying by our side, the fact was, she was a good girl, and everyone knew it. She couldn't be packaged as "Pretty Wild," because she just looked pretty young. I'm now horrified by some of things I did with her—posing topless at the dangerous Model Mayhem shoots my mom would send us to, doing drugs in front of her at clubs—forcing her into situations she never should have been in.

I had been protecting her my whole life, but now I was too fucked up to do even that.

One night, I came home and crawled in bed next to her. I was kicking dope and shaking and throwing up. I had just crawled my way to the bathroom, barely making it as I vomited across the bathroom floor. I looked up and there Gabby stood, still in her pajamas, like any normal 14-year old girl.

"Are you okay, Alexis?" she asked. I wasn't. I was so far from okay. I wanted to cry to my little sister, and tell her just how fucked up I was, how fucked up I had been my whole life. "I'll feel better in the morning," I promised. And I did. I called my dealer, picked up some Oxys and went back to living the double life Tess and I had perfected.

I was the scapegoat. Tess blew up the house and I was left to take care of the mess. But now, I couldn't even do that. It felt like everywhere I went was a disaster and Tess wasn't even there to blame. I didn't know how to take responsibility. I didn't know how to find my side of the street, let alone stay on it. All I could see was that my mom and dad had fucked me up, and this was their price to pay. I couldn't see that I was the one paying the steepest price. It was my soul I was selling, not theirs, but I couldn't see that when I woke up feeling like I wanted to die. I was the one poisoning me. I didn't understand that my parents didn't want to see me like that. I didn't understand that their hearts were broken, too.

Finally, one night, I'd had enough. My mom was mad that I had missed an audition. I was so tired of her demands and expectations, so I told her to go fuck herself. I grabbed my shit and decided I was going to run away. I called Tess, who invited me to stay at Nick's, where she was still living. But when I got there, she told me that she was going to spend the night with her boyfriend. I was so pissed. It was classic Tess. Right when I needed her most, she would bail on me for some dude.

Though I also had issues with codependency when it came to guys, Tess was always my first priority. I had been escaping through her for so many years, she was the one I needed most.

The whole summer was already feeling like a blur — caught between Xanax, Oxys and heroin. There were nights I didn't, and still don't, remember. Stories my sister would tell me later, and I'd ask, "Are you *sure* that happened?"

The night I drove over to Nick's was no different. I had already been high before getting into the fight with my mom, but now I was super loaded. I snorted a Xanax bar and smoked some Oxys before pulling up into Nick's driveway. I walked in and the party was already in full swing — everyone drinking and doing drugs. Someone suggested we head over to Beso, the restaurant where Tess ran up Neal Brennan's credit card.

"Sure," I shrugged, not knowing that my life was about to change forever.

## Chapter Eight

# The Bling Ring

*"Some changes look negative on the surface but*
*you will soon realize that space is being created*
*in your life for something new to emerge."*
—*Eckhart Tolle*

The shitty thing about being labeled a mastermind for something you didn't actually plan is that you kind of just wish you *were* the mastermind.

If I made the movie version of *The Bling Ring*, I would have fictionalized the story by turning myself into a cool *Ocean's 8*-type villain, except I would have robbed the rich to give to the poor (after getting my fair share of the drug money, of course). But that's not what happened, and that's not who I was.

The indisputable reality of it is that I was part of something terrible. It must have been so scary and violating for the victims that I can only imagine how it

felt. I've gotten adjacent enough to fame to understand when you don't feel safe anywhere. I know the
celebrities whose houses were burglarized lost more
than just material things, they were robbed of the one
safe place they had: their homes. I ended up carrying
the mantle of the ringleader while really just being
one of a number of co-defendants. Tess and I were
usually in the right place at the right time, but that
night I was in the wrong place at the wrong time.

So here's the truth. I've served my time; I have
nothing to hide. This isn't an attempt to minimize or
downplay what happened, but my role wasn't portrayed accurately in the media and it's my turn to
share my truth. For once in my life, the truth is a lot
more boring than fiction.

I wasn't really part of the Bling Ring gang. Although Nick was a friend of Tess', I didn't know him
that well. Our relationship only started a few months
prior, and really just consisted of getting fucked up.
Tess and Nick were like two peas in a pod, always
messing with me while I was wasted or passed out.
For example, one night after we'd all been drinking, I
came to in the back of Nick's car while they were slapping me in the face with burritos from Taco Bell. Super awesome. Tess was close with him and Nick was
obsessed with her. In one of his interviews with the
police, Nick said Tess had joined them on one of their
burglaries. But it was my name that ultimately became attached to the crime. I swear that if anyone had
told me where we were going that night, or what we
were going to be doing, I would have stayed home.

Not because I had some amazing moral code, but because I would have been terrified of getting caught. I was fine with smoking drugs and panhandling on the street, maybe even shoplifting, but this wasn't stealing some beer from Vons or mascara from Rite Aid. This was breaking and entering, going through people's belongings. This was some scary shit.

For decades, addicts have been criminalized. Drugs are illegal; therefore, if you use them you're a criminal. But I never thought of myself that way. I was just a good girl who had been through some really hard stuff, and the only way I knew how to feel better was to use. I didn't want to hurt anyone or steal from people. I knew what it felt like to be a victim and I always had a soft heart, even as my shell got harder and tougher. Just because I was addicted to opiates didn't mean I was okay with committing crimes. It just meant I was sick and I didn't know how to get better.

The night started out normally enough. We were at Beso drinking. I was already pretty wasted, and still pissed that Tess had ditched me and left me alone with Nick. He was a nice enough guy, but I barely knew him. I was also upset about the fight with my mom. We might have had our ups and downs, but we loved each other desperately. It wasn't until I got sober that I could see that love for the toxic bond that it was, but she was the only thing I had. Even if she made choices that I still don't agree with, I know she always genuinely loved me. To top it off, I couldn't believe that we were going through this right before we started shooting the pilot for our show. Things were going right. So why did everything still feel so fucked up? I didn't know.

I don't remember much from Beso. There was a bottle of vodka at the table and I was doing what I knew to do when I was upset: get high.

"We're gonna get going," Nick announced to me, after checking his phone and finishing his drink. I was nodding out on the long banquet table where we all had been sitting, and it wasn't clear that Nick was even inviting me along. He always seemed slightly annoyed by me. I think he was probably equally frustrated that Tess had left her junkie friend in his care.

"Okay," I mumbled.

"You wanna come?" he asked, as though he could care less whether I said yes or no, even though only hours before, he agreed I could stay with him. Plus, all my shit was still at his house. I don't know what else he expected me to do.

"Sure." I lifted myself up and lurched out after Nick, getting into the back seat of his Honda. I remember the blur of lights along Hollywood Boulevard as we drove in the opposite direction of his house.

"Are we going to a party?" I asked, staring out the window.

"Kind of. We're meeting some friends." Nick pulled up to a darkened house, where I saw people standing outside. I was having trouble talking, the drugs creating a dark haze in my head. Nick introduced me to his friend Rachel, who I recognized, because my ex-boyfriend Kevin cheated on me with one of her friends. I could barely get my name out so I didn't mention the connection. There was another friend of Nick's there, someone I had never met before. But no one seemed interested in getting to know each other.

"You got everything?" Rachel asked Nick.

"Stay here," Nick told me. He looked around, and I began to feel like we weren't going to a party. I hoped maybe they were just going inside to score drugs or something. I did a lot of sketchy things back then, but breaking and entering wasn't one of them. I stood outside for what seemed like forever. When you're loaded, you get bored easily. Plus, I was beginning to sober up, and I thought maybe they were getting high inside.

I was a zombie walking through life. I may have gotten the rep of being a criminal mastermind, but I was more like Scooby Doo. I went along with everyone else because I wanted to be loved. Tess was able to command people's attention. She was the leader and I had been following her for so long, that was all I knew how to do. I followed people until they hurt me too much, then I found someone else to follow. I didn't know how to lead. Even when I got sober, I followed my sponsor. I followed my husband. It wasn't until I became a mother that I became a leader. But that night, I followed Nick and Rachel right into that house, not knowing who it belonged to or what we were doing.

I walked up a big hill towards the house and squeezed through the gate, making my way through a yard and driveway, when I saw Nick running toward the front door. The house was being ransacked, and Nick and Rachel were stuffing clothes and watches and whatever else they could find into trash bags. I might have been high as a kite, but I knew what the fuck was happening. I knew what a robbery looked like.

I stood there like a deer in the headlights until Rachel shouted to Nick, "Give her a bag! At least she can help."

I was high. I had just been kicked out of my house. Tess and Nick were super close, and I didn't want to disappoint Tess's friend. There were so many factors overriding any normal moral reaction to the situation, I just did what I was told. I don't even remember what I put in the bag—some watches, a throw pillow, some scarves. It was like a bomb had gone off and we were taking from the wreckage.

All of sudden, Nick started yelling, "We got to go. We got to go!" as he barreled toward the front door. I ran with the bag that I had been slowly filling and followed them out into the street, jumping into Nick's car.

No one said anything the entire drive, not until we reached Nick's house. He turned to me with a dead look in his eye, "Don't you dare tell anyone about this." I nodded, more scared than I had been in my life. I felt totally sober, more sober than I had felt in years.

When we got inside, I went into the bathroom, and called my mom.

"Mommy," I cried. "It's really fucked up over here. I need to come home, please." My mom could hear the fear in my voice.

"Absolutely, baby. Come home right now." After everyone passed out, I slipped out of Nick's house, leaving behind the trash bag of random shit I had just stolen. I went home and never spoke to Nick Prugo or Rachel Lee again.

------------------------------------------------------------

## Chapter Nine

# Find the Glory in Your Story

*"Owning our story can be hard but not nearly as*
*difficult as spending our lives running from it.*
*Only when we are brave enough to explore the darkness*
*will we discover the infinite power of our light."*
— *Brené Brown*

"Hi, I'd like to report a robbery." I sat on the other end of the phone, my hand shaking as my mom sat in front of me. It had been over a month since the night of the burglary, but I couldn't wait any longer. I wanted someone to know what happened. I didn't know what else to say.

A few nights before, there had been a report on the news showing two figures running in the dark on a surveillance camera. The footage was from two robberies—one at Audrina Patridge's house, a cast member from the reality show *The Hills*, and the other from

Lindsay Lohan's house. I knew immediately who the two figures were: Nick and Rachel. As I quickly found out, they had been responsible for other burglaries as well. The list was long and, honestly, it made me embarrassed: Paris Hilton, Rachel Bilson, Brian Austin Green and Orlando Bloom.

We had just received the signed deal for *Pretty Wild* and our shooting schedule. Everyone was so excited, and I was scared one of my stupid decisions was going to ruin everything. The officer on the phone call asked when the robbery had taken place, but I couldn't offer him a date. I could barely figure out what day it was right then, let alone on a night where I was so high that I didn't realize I was in the middle of a robbery until people were throwing watches into trash bags.

"I'm not sure," I wavered. "Sometime last month?"

"Do you know the address of the incident?" the officer asked. He sounded annoyed, like I was playing a prank on him.

"I don't. But I think it was part of those celebrity robberies that they're showing on TV."

"Can I get your name and phone number?" he asked. I gave him my information, wanting to be helpful.

Then he asked, "Do you know who was responsible?" I hesitated, of course I knew. Though I had stayed away from Nick and Rachel, Tess was still living with Nick on and off. Was I really going to be responsible for getting him busted? I knew that shit was getting serious. But was I going to be the rat?

Me, the junkie/soon to be reality star? I had everything to lose, and nothing to gain. Plus, I hadn't forgotten the glint in Nick's eye when he told me not to tell anyone. I had already told my mom and Gabby. What would he do if he found out I told the police?

"Ma'am?" the man interrupted my silence. "Do you know the people responsible?"

Years later, I would realize that this might have been the beginning of my recovery journey because it was the first time my courage trumped my fear. I was honest. I told the truth, and I thought it would buy my freedom. I was scared of Nick and Rachel, but I was more scared of getting in trouble. My mom and I were finally getting a shot, and I didn't want to be the one to ruin it. It took everything in me to be honest.

"The people on the videos," I told the man, who I believed worked in the detective's unit. "I know them. Their names are Nick Prugo and Rachel Lee."

The officer asked for their contact information, but I told him I didn't have it. I was getting scared. Had I said too much? What would Nick do?

I hung up the phone and burst into tears. The officer told me that someone would be calling me back to follow up. Now, I was terrified. What had I just done?

"Don't worry," my mom promised me. "I'm sure they'll catch them." The thing was, neither my mom nor I thought I would get into trouble for the burglaries. I didn't know what Nick and Rachel were planning to do that night. I was barely there, and I left as soon as I could, never participating in another one.

How could I even be considered an accessory when I never wanted to be there?

I figured the police would call me back. When no one did, I actually tried to reach out to Lindsay Lohan's manager. It was like I was carrying around a terrible weight. The more people began to talk about these Hollywood bandits, the more I wanted to distance myself from what happened that night. I wanted to alert someone, anyone who might listen.

By the time September rolled around, we were focused entirely on the reality show. The name had changed from *Homeschooled with the Arlingtons* (my mom's fake last name) to *Pretty Wild*. Tess, Gabby, my mom and I couldn't wait. We really believed this would be our chance to show the world who we were. Although I was an 18-year old girl who had spent more time doing drugs than going to school, I thought I had something to say.

I was born with a sensitive heart that hardened from all the years of trauma. I always felt so connected to the pain of the world. I would cry watching the news, and I deeply wanted to be part of making the world a safer, healthier place. But how could an 18-year old junkie do that? I wasn't safe or healthy myself, but I knew that I had a purpose here. It wasn't just to go to clubs and get fucked up. I knew I had a story; I just didn't know exactly what it was yet or how to tell it.

The closer we got to the first day of principal shooting, the more drugs Tess and I used. That's the thing with substance abuse. It is often a system of self-sabotage. Looking back, it was like the closer I got to the thing I wanted, the stronger the pull away from it became. Somewhere deep in my body, there was a core belief that I didn't deserve happiness; that I wasn't worth it. Addiction is built to survive in this gap between who we want to be and who we believe we are. Like a parasite living off its host, it feeds off weaknesses. Tess and I were both getting high all day, every day, living off what was left from our signing bonus. I couldn't get through a day without opiates, whether that meant Oxys or heroin.

Finally, our first night of shooting arrived. The producers wanted to film us partying with the rapper Mickey Avalon, who was one of the first music acts discovered through Myspace. Mickey was famous for his heroin and crack use, so once the cameras were off, we were partying. We did Xanax and heroin all night, finally arriving home just as the sun was coming up.

For years, I was traumatized by what happened that day. It was hard for me to talk about it, remember it, to somatically re-experience the morning that changed my life forever. More often than not, it's hard to find the glory in the hard parts of life. We want to remember the times when we played the hero, but not the bad guy. But I eventually came to realize that even the worst parts of the past are opportunities for healing. The lessons we offer others so they can move through shame of their story, and instead, find the glory. Because the Divine is in each moment, even the worst.

I took another Xanax before passing out in my bed the minute my head hit the pillow. I was both exhausted and excited from the shoot and everything that was beginning to happen in our lives. Less than an hour later, I heard the banging on our front door. I thought I was dreaming. Really, it was just the beginning of my nightmare.

My mom answered the door, as police swarmed our house like a SWAT team. I woke up and realized what was happening, naively thinking that maybe they were just finally responding to my call from months earlier. But within minutes, I was standing there in shock holding a search warrant while they ransacked our home.

My mom was screaming, "What are you doing? What are you doing to us?" I was so high from the Xanax I just took, it felt like I couldn't move. I was a spectator; I wasn't there.

Here is the thing, trauma is trauma is trauma.

It's easy to say I brought it on myself. That I was just a dumb, young, spoiled drug addict who didn't give a shit about the world. But I was also an 18-year-old, who within minutes was watching her entire world torn apart because she partied with the wrong people one July night in 2009. I was scared shitless.

The police tore through my closet grabbing items of clothing that Nick Prugo had given me. I later found out the clothes actually belonged to Rachel Bilson. They dumped my jewelry onto the ground while Gabby cowered next to me. She was 16 and terrified.

Finally, one of the officers came over to me and said, "You're going to come with us to the station." Still wearing my pajamas, I nodded dutifully, believing that if I told the police what happened, they would understand. I had already called them after all. I wanted them to know I was innocent. I still didn't understand what was happening

As they led me to the cop car, I watched myself yell to my mom across our living room, where the camera crew was starting to set up, "Call the attorney!"

And that's the last thing I remember. Because once again, that age-old trauma set in, the type that forces our brain to protect us from our worst moments. Total system shut down. I don't remember the car ride or the interrogation. I know they kept feeding me information. At one point, they told me that the house I had been in belonged to Orlando Bloom. Later in the interrogation, they asked me whose house it was. I thought it was a quiz, and that I was supposed to get the right answer.

"Orlando Bloom?" I offered, hopefully. I could see them get excited. It was like the minute I mentioned the name, they were like, "We got you!" I was so confused. I all did was remember what they told me. I already told them everything I knew. I was the one who called and reported the crime in the first place.

Looking back now, it all makes so much more sense. They needed a culprit, and there I was. Young and naïve, in the middle of filming my reality show, and though they didn't drug test me, I am sure they could see I was fucked up. I was coming down from heroin and Xanax in the interrogation room; I just wanted to go home and crawl back to bed. Who cares about a dumb, young, spoiled drug addict who doesn't give a shit about the world? They certainly didn't.

Our society throws away its sick. Only recently, because of the opioid crisis, have some people begun seeing addiction for what it is: a survival mechanism for dealing with pain. But for years, we were stigmatized, driven underground, left to die. Even 10 years ago, there was little compassion. Addiction specialist Dr. Gabor Maté says that addicts are the scapegoats of our warped culture. *They're* the sick ones! The police didn't see a sick little girl who had made a very bad mistake. They saw a scapegoat—a role I had been playing my whole life.

As I found out later, Nick had identified me as being one of the two figures in the hazy security camera footage they had. They took us to the Van Nuys station for booking, and Rachel ended up in the car ride with me. We couldn't talk, and I'm not even sure what we would have said to each other. We were both in our own worlds of mayhem. It was just for one night, but those worlds intersected.

And now, it was like I could never get out.

Despite my addiction, I had never actually been in trouble with the law. I once got busted by a cop for having weed, but he just threw it out and sent me on my way. Now, I was getting printed and photographed and walked to a cell where a bunch of women stood around, impatient, angry and bored. Years later,

I actually began researching how the criminal justice system works, but I didn't need a PhD to see immediately that prisons turn their backs on the poor. I was the only white girl in the room. And certainly one of the only women who could make a phone call and be out in hours. Most of the prisoners were waiting for family to find a bondsman, to somehow put together the money to post bail. Most of them were in there for crimes related to their poverty, something they had to do to support their habits or their families and they were too poor to get out. There are a lot of people making a lot of money off of this system. I was one of the lucky ones, but more than that, I was privileged by my economic status and the color of my skin. My mom posted my bail, and within hours, she came to get me.

As we were walking down the hallway, she warned me, "There are a lot of photographers out there."

While I had been in the jail cell, the gossip sites were going crazy with the story—the celebrity burglars were caught, and one of them was a reality star! Even though we had just begun to shoot the pilot.

My mom had always told us, "Don't do anything so bad that it can land you on the cover of the *LA Times*." And there I was, on the cover of nearly every news publication.

Be careful what you put out there. What I now understand is that we are the ultimate creators of our own story. I don't mean that in a *The Secret*, manifestation sort of way. I mean that how we view ourselves will always be reflected in the story we share with the world. When we tap into our glory, our story shifts. We don't suck the light out of the world but instead the light shines out of us and into it. My story was creating darkness because I could only see the darkness in myself. I was losing the light, and so I found myself on the cover of the *LA Times* as a notorious criminal.

As soon as I got home, I went back to bed. Our show producer Dan had already called us. He and the other producer were shocked, but also thrilled by the news. After all, this was good TV. They wanted to refilm me being arrested. So the day *after* cops burst into my home, ransacked all my belongings and led me away in handcuffs, we did it all again, but with actors, lights and cameras rolling. Talk about being re-traumatized. Of course, we went along with it. I was now facing burglary charges. We believed that the show could save us. And we weren't wrong. With us all over the news, the pilot got picked up by E!, who ordered an entire first season.

Now we had money to pay for my legal problems. And I had money to pay for my addictions.

But as I was about to find, both were about to get much, much worse.

## Chapter Ten

# How Far You Want to Fall?

*"If you want a new outcome, you will have to break the habit of being yourself, and reinvent a new self."*
—Joe Dispenza

Some say we get to choose our own bottoms. We decide how low we want to go. Others call it the dark night of the soul. A place through which you don't know how you will possibly pass, or whether you will survive at all. We are all faced with the question, how far can I fall? It seems like the wider the net, the lower we can go. The fewer consequences there are for our behaviors, the less likely we are to cry, "Mercy!" Then there are times when we know the end is near, but all we can say is, "Not. Fucking. Yet."

After the arrest, we started filming season one of *Pretty Wild*, and to say it was pretty wild would be an understatement. I was getting up at 5 am to shoot.

When the cameras were on, we were doing spray tans and mani-pedis and trips to Mexico. And then when the cameras were off, all I did was smoke pills to numb out.

 None of it felt real.

That's what I found out. When it comes to reality TV, none of it *is* real.

We were given a plan for each scene. Our lives were engineered for maximum on-screen drama. We were forced to fight to keep the show interesting, when really, all I wanted to do was run away and sleep forever.

Instead, I found myself abusing everyone around me, and abusing myself. Worse, the fights that were created for the show didn't end when the filming did. We were all pushed to say and do terrible things to the people we loved and became complicit. We crossed lines. That didn't just disappear when the director yelled cut. Instead, we returned to real life with new resentments and injuries.

In order to produce drama, we created trauma. We built up these episodes on real things, on real issues from our pasts—conflicts, fear and fights. And everything was raw for me emotionally. Not only were we pinning all our hopes on this show that was slowly poisoning all of us, but as my lawyer explained, I was now facing real jail time. It felt like my entire life had led to this moment, and now this moment might lead me to jail. Every day was so intense, and I didn't know how to handle it. I didn't know how to do anything but get worse.

On top of it, my newfound notoriety made me feel like I was being watched all the time, which really sucks when you're a drug addict just trying to score. Tess and I were still panhandling for money to buy drugs, even as we were filming a reality show for a popular cable network and I was facing first-degree burglary charges. On our show, we all lived in a beautiful fake home that overlooked the Hollywood Reservoir, but at night, Tess and I would return to our real home—a small room we shared at the Best Western on Franklin Avenue in Hollywood, just off the 101 Freeway.

It seemed like the closer Tess and I got to success, the sicker our relationship became. Our friendship had long been more like an addiction to one another, and now it mirrored our actual addictions. The two things were becoming one. We were experts at using people to get what we wanted from them, but now, we had a new, elevated platform with which to do that. We were on TV. It's amazing and horrible what opportunities appearing on TV can afford two girls just looking to get high. When you're using drugs, you build a little family of users and dealers and barter with whatever you have—cash, drugs, your body—to get what you need. But now, Tess and I had fame. And we started using it to get whatever we wanted.

We met this finance guy who would take us to Bloomingdale's and spend thousands of dollars on us. We didn't even have to sleep with these men. We just had to make them think there was a possibility.

Just the promise of our bodies was enough to score us drugs, clothes and cash. And Gabby was often along for the ride.

She was still just a teenager, and we took her places she didn't belong. There was one photo shoot that haunts me to this day, where they wanted us to act very inappropriate, jumping through the air with scarves. I didn't want to do it, but Gabby did...and I let her. She was only 15. In so many ways, I thought of myself as her mother, and yet, here I was, stealing her childhood just as mine had been stolen. They say the victim can become the perpetrator, and though I probably loved her more than anyone on the planet, I didn't protect her. Not the way I wanted to and the way she deserved to be—if not by a parent, by someone. She became collateral damage of my addiction.

It says somewhere in the book *Alcoholics Anonymous* that hitting bottom is losing the one thing you love and still not being able to stop. I knew I had betrayed Gabby, I was betraying my whole family. Worst of all, I had betrayed myself and I couldn't stop. We met with the lawyer and I barely heard him. That's the thing about falling. It looks really fast to everyone else, but when you're the one hitting bottom, it feels like everything is happening in slow motion. I was swimming in mud, and I didn't even recognize myself anymore.

Whatever made me fun or interesting in the first place, was fading fast. All the parts of me that once made Tess and I the life of the party—the combination of that light we all have, mixed with survival skills and a solid dash of the magic that happens when the drugs hit those opiate receptors—was burning out. As my spark dwindled, my anger at Tess only increased. She was the one who introduced me to Nick, yet here I was. The one facing jail time, not her.

Tess was so fucked up she could barely show up for our shoots. But what did she have to lose? She was still free.

I had so much on the line that I was determined to be professional. I convinced myself that they couldn't possibly send me to jail if I had a hit TV show. Right? But Tess hated getting up early for shooting days. In Mexico, when we ran out of drugs halfway through the trip, we were so dope sick that she refused to film. This made the producers insane.

I was so consumed by fear, addiction and anger, all I could do was crush drugs and smoke them. Foil, then eventually a needle, was my solution to every problem. I felt like I was decaying on the inside, and I didn't care. What were my other options? It never occurred to me that I deserved a better life, that I was capable of so much more. Every time I went to court, I had our own camera crew with me, plus outside media. It was a circus, and all so traumatic. The feedback loop was turned up to 11.

I just wanted someone to stop it all, make the cameras go away, the court hearings stop. I wanted someone to protect me. But once again, the people that should have been doing that were more focused on how they could profit from the situation. I was being re-traumatized in my trauma. Back to being five years old, being abused and taken advantage of, while the ones assigned to protect me failed to intervene.

My mom should have seen what the show was doing to me, and considered how it might influence the case. She should have pulled the plug, but naively, she thought we would come off as "good guys" to the public. I guess we should have all known that reality shows aren't there to show people's character assets.

Reality TV is really just a modernized version of the Roman gladiators—humans forced to battle each other for the audience's delight, especially when it involves young girls or women. It's our society's shadow on full display. And yet, we still don't see it for what it is. My mom somehow thought, maybe because we were so young, that this time would be different.

It wasn't.

We began to get media requests from big publications that wanted exclusive interviews. My lawyer was strict when it came to outside media. "No talking to the tabloids" was the very first piece of advice he had for me. But when *Vanity Fair* reached out to do a piece on what the writer, Nancy Jo Sales, referred to as the "Bling Ring"—a term that will follow me for the rest of my life—we thought it was finally a shot at redemption. Sales seemed so sympathetic. She said she was a mother herself, and acted as though she understood my relatively small part in the whole case. She empathized with the fact my recent shot at reality fame made me a target of the media and the police.

I really do hesitate to diminish my role in the Bling Ring, though my account might seem otherwise. I don't expect people to believe me, and I don't need them to, now that it's all over. In fact, I know some people may never believe me. In fact, I had a lively text conversation with Nancy Jo Sales recently, agreeing to disagree on what happened that night. But this is my opportunity to describe what happened from my point of view, and I'll take it.

We believed there were injustices committed during the investigation and thought that Sales was there to help us clear up the confusion, that the *Vanity Fair* piece would not only prove my innocence to the world, but to the court. When the piece came out, it was horrifying. She painted me as a "fame monster" that only cared about partying. In reality, I was the one who felt so guilty I called the police months before my arrest. But that was not how Sales described me. She seemed more concerned with what shoes we were wearing, than what was actually happening in our lives. She now infamously reported that I was wearing expensive six-inch Louboutins, which were actually little Bebe heels. There's a big difference not just in price, but in perception.

I know the scene of me reading the article and irately calling Sales to give her a piece of my mind has launched a million memes, and I can finally laugh at it, too. But the footage didn't just show an oblivious, entitled girl yelling about Bebe heels, it showed a young woman with substance use disorder hitting her bottom, screaming into the void.

How easy is it to laugh at people when they're down? We all point fingers at the fallen, and sometimes it is well deserved (Harvey Weinstein, I'm looking at you). But often, it's just people going through the worst days of their life while everyone watches. No one has much compassion for when you're losing your mind. They love you when you're on the other side, sharing about how you got it back. But no one loves you when you're in the middle of your shit. And I was in the middle of my shit.

The scene where I'm frantically trying to record the perfect angry voicemail for Nancy Jo Sales, screaming "Every time you yell, I have to fucking re-record it!" at my mom, pretty much sums up our relationship back then.

I also see something else in that scene. I see a scared little girl, who has just been painted as a rich, spoiled brat who motivated a spree of burglaries. I see a drug addict who is terrified to go to jail, who doesn't know how she's going to get through a day, let alone years, without getting high. I see a daughter and a sister who are afraid they're going to take her away from her family. I see someone who feels betrayed by the one person she thought was finally going to help protect her.

And I see somebody who so, so badly needed help.

Instead, I was portrayed to the world as someone people *wanted* to go to jail, someone who deserved her comeuppance. Again, it's that gladiator aspect of our culture, the sadistic desire to see the screws turn for someone who's already suffering. Particularly when they represent something we don't like for whatever reason—whether it's about warped values or something we can't accept about ourselves.

So I screamed and ranted about Bebe shoes and made reality TV history. The next month, when I went to court and my lawyer told me to take a plea deal, I didn't know what else to do.

As he explained, "If Orlando Bloom testifies against you, it's going to look so bad."

He kept telling me it was the best thing for me and my family. All I could think of was Gabby. How much more could I continue to hurt her? How much more of her childhood had to be destroyed because of my fuck ups?

My attorney looked me dead in the eye and said, "This is the best thing you can do for yourself."

When we don't believe in ourselves, we will believe what other people believe. We will see the worst that they see in us. It's called the "Looking Glass Self Theory." Though I knew I was so much more genuine than the picture painted by Sales in *Vanity Fair* and I knew I was so much more innocent than the picture painted by the courts, I could only mirror what other people projected. I was locked in so tightly to my role. I had nothing left. I couldn't improvise my way out. The bottom was coming closer and the girl I had become was about to be obliterated. Of course, it turned out that was the good news. But I didn't know that yet.

I refused to plead guilty because I didn't *feel* guilty. Not fully. I stood there with a trash bag, sure. I did what they asked me, threw some stuff in it because I was stoned and terrified. But my intentions weren't there. I didn't want to be in that house any more than Orlando Bloom wanted me to be there.

So I pleaded no contest.

Then I got high and waited to be sentenced.

## Chapter Eleven

---

# Consequences

*"I do not understand the mystery of grace —*
*only that it meets us where we are and*
*does not leave us where it found us."*
*—Anne Lamott*

On June 24, 2010, I turned myself into the criminal courts building in downtown Los Angeles. It was four days after my 19th birthday.

One year earlier, we had been in the middle of selling the pitch to our show. I had just turned 18; my career was on the rise. We thought we were about to be the Kardashians. And now, here I was shuffling into jail wearing an orange jumpsuit, terrified about what was going to happen to me. We filmed up until the moment when I turned myself in. Then I was on my own, in a way I had never been before.

I lost all my freedoms the minute they booked me. I had no say in anything. Maybe I should have expected that, but the idea of jail is not the same as the real thing. You have no idea what's it's really like until you're there. It's more like a feeling than anything else. You can imagine what you've seen on TV or in the movies. You can get scared about being raped in the bathroom or eating disgusting prison food, but none of that really matters in there. Maybe what hurts the most is that no one cares.

No one in there cared whether I was comfortable, whether I was burning hot or if I was freezing cold. They certainly didn't care if I was safe.

I was put in a holding cell. I was a child in a room of adult women in downtown LA. Just like the first time I was arrested, I was the only white woman there.

There's no way to prepare yourself for the absolute inequity of prison. Robert Downey, Jr. once said something like, "You can't go to prison and come out a liberal." I have no idea what he meant, because I left with the seeds of the social justice warrior I currently aspire to be planted in me. All I saw in there was how our criminal system was a cruel, brutally racist attack on people with so much less than me.

Sure, people had done bad things. Some of the women were charged with terrible, violent crimes but I had to wonder, how many of them had suffered the same or worse violations than I had? How many had endured severe pain as little girls? Except unlike me, they usually weren't serving six-month sentences.

They were serving years while they awaited trial, many because they couldn't afford bail.

Prison was developed to punish people for bad deeds. As someone who has been on the receiving end of bad deeds, I understand the intention. The problem is, the system ends up imprisoning the people who can't get out of their own mistakes and lets the ones who can buy their freedom go free. Justice isn't fair when it only serves a few. And I saw firsthand how unjust our system is. How my molester could be free and how women who were just along for the ride were serving life.

I made my way to the corner of the room, not realizing there was a toilet there. I sat down just as a woman took a huge shit next to me. All I could do was accept that this was my fate. After a few hours, they passed out a bagged lunch of bologna sandwiches before putting us all on a bus. I found out then that you don't talk about why you're there, and you never, ever say you're guilty. Because people could use information against you to reduce their own time.

In a way, being a drug addict prepared me for this. What I wasn't prepared for, though, was detoxing in jail.

I wish I'd had the ability to plan ahead and detox before arriving, but I was an addict. I used up to the last minute before walking in, and that high held through the first few hours. By the time we arrived at Lynwood Female Correctional Facility, I was beginning to feel the early symptoms of dope sickness, which would eventually lead to full-blown withdrawal. They made me strip down in front of the cops and bend over and cough. I wished I had been smart enough to bring drugs in with me. Instead, I was just beginning to feel that cold trickle of anxiety move through my nervous system.

Because of the media circus around my arrival, they decided I needed to be put in protective custody. They gave me my uniform and my rollup pad, with a blanket (no pillow), and led me down a cold, barren hallway. Finally, they opened up one of the pods. The women inside were all still asleep, so I tried to walk quietly to the only open cell.

The pod contained six cells up top and six on the bottom, and one shower, which smelled like the toilet in our cells. Because I thought, naively, they would give us water with our meals; I didn't drink any for the first few days. All I had was the small trickle of water that came from the sink.

Soon, all I could do was throw up. I was projectile vomiting in the toilet, on the floor, in my bed. I tried to keep down the milk and juice they gave us with our meals, but I was too sick. I'm not sure there is a worse hell than an opiate detox in prison. You have nothing to look forward to; there is no easy comfort and no way out. I had been escaping my whole life, and now I was truly imprisoned, literally. The withdrawals only made the walls thicker. It felt like I would never see the people I loved again. Since getting sober, I have struggled with depression. I have woken up with the feeling like everything is doomed and the sky is falling. But when you're detoxing from dope in jail, everything *really is* doomed. The sky is actually falling.

The other women felt bad for me, but as I found out, pity doesn't buy you much in jail.

I've considered writing a book, *Jail for Dummies*, because I had no idea how to take care of myself in there. Something like that would have been extremely valuable. Finally, one of the women asked if I had any money on my books, so I could buy some food and supplies from the commissary. I had no clue how all that worked. She was the Mama of the cellblock, explaining to me that I could get some things I might need to make it all easier.

"You're sick, baby," she shook her head, looking at the vomit on the wall of my bunk. "You don't want to be sick in here."

The next time we were allowed to make a call, I told my mom what to do so I could have a little money. The next day, I was able to buy shower shoes, bottled water, and Snickers bars. I hadn't taken a shower in days because I had barely been able to stand up, but the withdrawal was finally starting to subside. I will never forget that first, cold, hard shower. It felt like it was the first time I'd been awake in years. The only problem was, I was waking up in jail.

A number of people wrote me when I was in jail, friends and fans of the show, and I was so grateful. I was able to get a pencil and paper from the commissary and I wrote them back. I started to feel like a human again.

In so many ways, I hadn't had human contact in years, and through their letters, I was connecting again. I was feeling alive, even if I had no idea where my life was going. I had been checking out since childhood. It was how I survived what had happened to me—I would get high and avoid whatever consequences I was rotting in. I would ignore my reality even as I filmed a reality show.

Jail is perhaps one of the most emotionally sobering places on earth because there is nothing there to distract you. Sure, there was a TV in the main room, but usually the toughest women ran the control and they had the worst taste in shows. And you could barely see it anyway through the small rectangular piece of thick plexiglass on your cell door. It was just me and my reality, no TV. I was staring right into all the choices I had made, but also the choices that had been made for me. And I didn't have any Oxy or heroin to escape them.

Life is full of discomfort. It's hard, and sometimes it can all be just too much. I felt like I'd spent my whole life dodging slings and arrows. What I realized after I got sober was that I would never experience true happiness until I was willing to walk through the pain.

I had no choice but to accept the pain in prison, and I learned to be absolutely present in the moment because of it.

Though we always think of "being present" as some great spiritual goal, it can also be really fucking hard. Because tough shit happens in the present.

Recently, I've been dealing with some financial insecurities and some medical anxieties. There will always be a part of me that doesn't want to be there for the hard stuff, but I learned that I could never grow until I was willing to stretch. And I had been shrinking for long enough.

Before going to jail, the sentence sounded like forever, but the time ticked by. I would get out once a day to shower and make a quick phone call.

They say that the absence of touch can cause insanity. In an experiment, baby monkeys died when they didn't receive physical contact from their mothers. We are deeply social beings. I couldn't even imagine what those women with years of time ahead of them felt like. After 48 days, thankfully, I didn't have to.

One evening, I was called down to the main station over the loud but muffled PA system. I could barely make out my name but jumped up. The guards told me to bring my belongings, but they didn't say why. I walked with the guard through the multiple layers of doors and pods, as we made our way through protective custody. I had no idea what was happening; I thought maybe I was just moving cells.

I was standing in a row with two other girls, holding all the things that I'd just bought from commissary.

"You can't take that stuff," the guard told me.

I started getting frustrated and said, "But I just bought all of this!"

One of the other girls stopped me. "You don't need that shit. You're getting out."

I couldn't believe it. Even as they gave me a plastic bag containing the outfit I had come in with, and I walked out into the dark to greet my family. My mom, stepdad and sister, Gabby, were waiting for me, with a group of photographers standing behind them. I'm not sure my mom called them, but I pulled my hoodie around my face and rushed toward my parents. I didn't want to be famous. I just wanted to go home.

Ironically, I never made it home that night. I went to In-N-Out with my family, and then I used my mom's phone to call a friend who was having a party at her house.

Now, most parents would have said, "No way! You just got out of jail, you're coming home for a hot shower and home-cooked meal." But that wasn't my family; it had never been my family. It was cheese-burgers and see you later. I understand that they were also scared. They didn't know what to say or how to comfort me. None of us ever thought I would one day be sentenced to jail for robbery. My mom had pre-pared herself for awards ceremonies, not for jail time.

So after we ate, they drove me to my friend's house, and handed me a key to an apartment my mom had rented for me while I was in jail. I had never been there before, so she wrote down the address of my new home on a scrap of paper. It was so trippy being out. I could go where I wanted, do what I wanted, eat what I wanted and use whatever I wanted. I was terrified to go to sleep that night be-cause I thought I would wake up and it would all be a dream, that I would be back in jail. So instead, I went to my friend's and got blackout drunk.

After feeling entirely present and awake for a month, I did the only thing that seemed to make sense and the only thing I was any good at: check back out. I now understand why people leave jail and end up right back where they started. Because you're not prepared at all. You're released back to the old friends, the old ways and the old survival mechanisms, and all you know how to do is survive, even if that means a one-way ticket back to jail.

Because in its own way, prison is safe. The other people might be dangerous (and they're a lot less dangerous than the TV shows depict) but if you're in jail, the most dangerous person you know is probably yourself. Prison protects you from you. It protects you from temptations and worst impulses. I had been looking for someone to protect me my whole life. In jail I finally felt safe. I felt free from the harm I might inflict upon myself.

But now, I was back in my old prison and the walls were far more impenetrable. The worst part was, I was serving my own life sentence, with no end in sight. And I had no idea how to get out. I didn't realize the key was inside me the whole time.

## Chapter Twelve

# Own Your Shit

*"Our deepest fear is not that we are inadequate.*
*Our deepest fear is that we are powerful beyond measure.*
*It is our light, not our darkness that most frightens us.*
*Actually, who are you not to be? You are a child of God.*
*Your playing small does not serve the world."*
—Marianne Williamson

I stood by myself in my new apartment. I was completely wasted and completely alone. I got in the shower and sat under the hot water for what seemed like hours, thinking. I was 19 years old, just hours out of prison and already back to using.

How did I get here?

While I was in prison, I gave Tess all the money I had left from the show to pay our rent on the apartment we shared. Instead, she shot up the money, and got us kicked out. My mom had cleared all of my things out of that place and found a sad little studio apartment off of Burbank Boulevard for me instead. I actually had to change units in the building at one point because the first apartment was infested with wasps. Every time I drive into the city, I still see the place, backing right up to the 12 lanes of the I-5 Freeway.

I was grateful my mom found me a place to live, but it also reminded me of how much I'd lost.

I hadn't called Tess in weeks, since finding out about the money and our former apartment. For years, it was so easy to blame my troubles on Tess. I felt like I could trace everything back to her—the drug use, my failure to show up for life, even the burglary. Our relationship had consumed me for decades, and I just couldn't pull us apart anymore. I didn't know where friendship ended and codependency began.

In all that toxicity, I couldn't find myself.

I wasn't able to own my shit because I had always looked to Tess for the answer. Instead of discovering my own "why," I just asked "how?" I was so focused on "How did I get here?" that I failed to ask myself "Why did I get here?" Because "how" is just a list of events, but "why" is a series of emotions and attitudes. And it was my own emotions and attitudes that brought me to that tiny apartment in Burbank, sobbing under a hot shower.

My mom checked in with me daily, making sure I got to my probation meetings. Though we didn't talk about my using, she reminded me that I wanted to be healthy for the show. The first season had wrapped, and we were convinced that we'd received enough media attention to warrant being renewed for a second.

At that time, being better meant staying away from Tess. I knew she was using dope, and that she was starting to get into needles. I hadn't yet tried IV drugs. We had both preferred to snort and smoke our pills and heroin. Maybe it gave us an illusion of being better than we were. So knowing that Tess was now using intravenously made me extra cautious about spending time with her.

Then we found out that the show was cancelled. I will never forget how upset my mom was; it was like she just lost her life's savings.

I was bummed, too.

Like my mom, I didn't really understand the reason for the show's cancellation. We had millions of viewers each week. I had received countless letters (handwritten, mailed letters back then) from people saying how much they loved the show. But I also couldn't help but feel relieved. If anyone had been embarrassed by the show, it was me. I was the one who was on trial. I was the one who went to jail. I was the one whose embarrassing voicemail—horrifying really—was heard around the world.

Yet this job was not only paying our bills, but also for my drug habit.

Oddly enough, news of the cancellation is what brought Tess and I back together again.

Tess was less bitter about it. She'd hated all the schedules and rules and demands. Plus, whatever dreams she'd had of being one of Hef's Playmates seemed like a distant memory. Her primary purpose was now to get high.

My mom became determined for me to rebuild my life without *Pretty Wild*. "There's no reason you can't keep modeling," she told me.

"Um, yes there is," I replied. "I've been to jail."

"So has Lindsay Lohan," my mom reminded me. Coincidentally enough, Lohan had served her own jail sentence around the same time I did, and in the same place, Lynwood Correctional Facility, just a few cells down. But my career was in a very different place than Lohan's in 2010. I was a small-time reality star, best known for going to jail. Lohan was still one of the biggest actresses on the planet. I didn't even bother responding to my mom. I just wanted to disappear.

Which is what Tess and I got to work doing.

Only a matter of days after the show got cancelled Tess called me and said her boyfriend was being mean to her. I had been attempting to only drink and smoke pot to stay "'healthy" for the show. But by the time I picked Tess up that night, I had nothing left, physically, financially or spiritually. There was nothing "healthy" about me. I told her that she couldn't smoke dope around me, but later that evening, I walked in on her holding a flame under the foil, smoking heroin.

It was game over for me.

I took the tooter from her hands and had my first hit in more than 60 days. The wave washed over me and I went underneath. I was at the bottom of the sea.

Getting high was the only place where I experienced peace. It's why so many people confuse drugs with a spiritual experience. And in their own way, they are one and the same. Because when that first high hits you, you feel like God is holding you. You feel present and perfect and like everything is going to be okay. Even as your world is crashing down around you. I was drowning, and it felt so fucking good.

The following week, I followed Tess to the needle for the first time. We were hanging out at our dealer's apartment and he started cooking some heroin for me to shoot up. At this point, we were already back to doing anything for the drugs. We would do "favors" for our drug dealers. We would do "favors" for their friends. Anything to keep the supply coming.

I had stopped going to my probation meetings because I was too fucked up. If they knew I was using, I would be sent back to jail. I failed to put two and two together, that not showing up was basically the same thing as checking in fucked up. I was already a month behind in rent. I knew they would be kicking me out of my apartment soon.

Overwhelmed doesn't begin to describe my state. It was more like a rapture of the deep, the last feeling, one of profound peace, that one feels right before they drown.

What did it matter if we shot up? What did I have to lose?

Our drug dealer, Cole, was renting a room from a friend, and all three of us were sitting on his bed. I gave him my arm, and felt the burning shot go into my veins. Within seconds, I felt it hit my stomach, as I ran to the bathroom to puke. I cleaned myself up just as our dealer was lining Tess up with a shot.

"That made me so fucking sick," I shared with the group, slumping back down on the bed.

"It's cool," he smiled as he tied up Tess' arm.

"I put a little speed in yours," he told Tess. A lie it would turn out.

Tess grinned, like she was getting the special dose and I just got the shit shot.

Cole leaned forward and slipped the needle into her arm, and instantly I watched her eyes roll into the back of her head and her body go straight and stiffen.

"Holy shit, holy shit," I began to yell. "What's wrong with her?"

"Shhhh, shut the fuck up," Cole hissed, afraid we were going to wake up his roommate. "She'll be fine."

But Tess started to turn purple. She was far from fine.

"The fuck, Cole? We need to call 911."

"Uh-uh, not here, you're not. Fuck that." I can't even begin to tell you how many of us die because of conversations exactly like this. I was still high from my dose, but the adrenaline kicked in, and it was like I became Super Sober. Everything went clear as a bell. Tess, Cole, the room. The world started to move in slow motion as I slapped Tess to wake her up. But she wouldn't come to. I grabbed Tess' limp body and with whatever strength I had, dragged her from the house and threw her in the passenger seat of my car.

I didn't know what to do or where to go, but I just started driving, trying to figure out my way to the closest hospital. I was trying to call 911 when she started throwing up. Afraid she was going to choke on her own vomit, I pulled over and dragged her out onto the sidewalk. I was attempting CPR when a cop saw us and called an ambulance. The ambulance arrived in minutes, while I was still holding Tess in my lap. The cop kept asking what was wrong with her.

I just told him that I didn't know. That we'd been at a party and I'd found her this way.

The medics finally arrived and quickly determined that she was overdosing. They administered Narcan and Tess came back to life.

The police officer asked what she had taken.

"It was just my Adderall," she lied. "I think I took too much of it."

I'm not sure why the cop didn't question us further. I'm not sure why the medics didn't make us go to the hospital. I'm not sure why, at the very least, the cop didn't search our car, where he would have quickly found coke and weed and Oxys.

Instead, an hour after Tess almost died at the corner of Winnetka and Oxnard, we got in my car and drove back to my studio apartment in silence. We swore we would never do it again, but a couple of weeks later, we were back at the same dealer's house with needles in our arms.

I didn't know how to stop, but even worse, I didn't want to stop. I didn't want to look at what a mess I was making of my life, so instead, I just made a bigger mess to cover it up. It's like when my kids are looking for a toy and they pull every other toy out of the box. They can never find what they're looking for in the mayhem; they just make a bigger disaster. I didn't know how to own my shit; I just knew how to escape from it. And as the stakes got higher—the threat of eviction, of more jail time—as I became less able to live in reality, escaping was becoming less of an option, too.

Not long after, Tess got back together with her boyfriend. It was the usual pattern with us: she would break up with her guy and come running to me, we would start partying together and I would help her pick up the pieces. Then, inevitably, she would return to the guy, and I would feel abandoned once again. I would refuse to speak to her until the next breakup, when we would repeat the vicious cycle again.

I had been out of jail since August, and it was now November. In three short months, everything had fallen apart. I couldn't pay any of my bills. I was stealing checks from my mom and cashing them just to pay for my drug habit. I was back to panhandling at gas stations and spending the night with whatever drug dealer would get me high.

One day, my mom checked in on me in our little apartment. She noticed that there were boxes of aluminum foil all over the place, some empty, some not.

"Alexis, what are all these rolls of foil for?"

How dare she ask me that, I thought. I seethed at her, "I like to bake, you cunt."

My mom begged me to get help, but none of us really understood what help meant. One day, Gabby found heroin in my purse when she was looking for a lighter. She held up the baggie of black tar for me to see.

"What is this?" she asked as I snatched it from her hands.

"You know what it is," I snapped. "And don't fucking say anything."

Though I still had my apartment, I wasn't paying any of the bills. There was no electricity and no heat, so a lot of nights, I would go back to my mom's to sleep, no matter how fucked up I was. Because although my mom had her faults, she always let me in.

Now I understand, even at 19, I was her baby girl. She just wanted to know I was safe. And every morning I woke up alive and under her roof was a fucking miracle.

We both knew it.

One day, I went out with a friend, and we ended up shooting dope together. He dropped me off around midnight. I crawled into bed next to Gabby. I was beginning to kick, but I knew it would be worse when I woke up. I had a little bit of heroin left on me (.08 grams to be exact) so I figured I would hang onto it, to use in the morning before my dealer started taking calls.

I could hear Gabby snoring softly. Her warm body safely asleep next to me.

I didn't want to be like this anymore, but I didn't understand that I had a choice. All I knew was how to get high. I hadn't done any work around healing. Sure, my mom had sent us to therapists and holistic healers, even ashrams, but I had never been willing to be honest, to really reveal my pain. I knew how to point my finger at other people, but I didn't know how to look at the girl in the mirror.

I passed out next to my sister with only one thing in mind—calling my dealer as soon as possible.

This time, I didn't hear the cops knocking on the front door. I didn't even realize they were in the house until they were standing over Gabby and me, my mom calling out and crying from behind them.

"Leave her alone! Don't you think she's been through enough?"

A female officer stood over me, showing her badge. "Alexis Neiers?" she asked.

"Huh?"

"We're here on a probation violation..."

"What?" I began to wake up. "I haven't done anything."

Another cop was already looking around the room when he noticed my purse. I saw him walking toward it, so I hollered at him, struggling to get out of bed, "That's not mine!"

Probably not the most innocent sounding thing to say when someone is about pull heroin out of your bag.

They found the .08 grams.

"That's not mine!" I declared once again. I tried to search for a lie, any lie and I found the worst one I could say. "It's hers!"

I pointed to Gabby—this sweet, confused girl who had just been woken up from her warm sleep and was now being accused by her junkie sister of having heroin in her purse.

"What?" Gabby was dumbfounded.

My mom jumped in. "That's not true. Gabby doesn't do drugs."

My lie was short-lived. They found my wallet and ID in the same purse. It was clear who the heroin belonged to. My story did nothing but make me look and feel worse.

Once again, I was led out of my mom's house in handcuffs, a little over a year after the first arrest. Because it was a Friday, they couldn't transfer me to Lynnwood. Instead, they took me to the Lost Hills Sheriff's station in Calabasas for the weekend.

My mom called our attorney and they tried to figure out what they could do.

By the time I made it to the Sheriff's station, I began to go into withdrawal. I was shivering, shaking and vomiting the whole weekend. The worst part about heroin is that you think after the first two days, you'll get better, like with food poisoning. But actually, the first couple of days are just the beginning. It's on days three, four and five that you really want to die.

On Monday morning, they transferred me back to Lynnwood. By that point, I had no control over my intestines. I was vomiting and had diarrhea. Within hours of moving to my cellblock, I shit my pants. I wasn't scheduled to get a fresh pair until the next day, and I had already missed the daily shower.

In case anyone needs a clear picture of how bad it got for me that was it. Welcome to hitting bottom.

I kept calling out to the guards that I was dying, but they had seen plenty of women detox in jail before. I wasn't going to get any special privileges for being on the E! network. No one wanted to get anywhere near me.

Finally, one of the other girls gave me an extra sheet she had so I could clean myself up. I curled up on my tiny, painfully thin sleeping pad, and knew there was nothing I could do but wait it out.

The next week, I finally got my day in court. I was nine days into my detox and I was still shivering and sweating. I had been getting high every day for months, and I had never felt worse in my life.

Instead, all I could do was wait for the ride to be over.

That day, my new attorney, Mike Nasatir, a wonderful man who to this day, I credit for teaching me what it means to be an adult, sat me down and told me I had two options:

"Alexis, you can either take responsibility for your life and beg for the mercy of the courts," he told me. "Or you can spend six years in prison."

You think that would have been an easy choice. They say you can ask an addict if they would rather get sober and live a life beyond their wildest dreams, or stay loaded and risk ending up in jail or dead, and the addict will almost always reply, "Can you give me a minute?"

I needed a minute.

Mike, a gentle and patient man with the kindest eyes you've ever seen, nodded.

"So will I have to admit to the heroin?" I asked.

"Yes. Or you can go to prison." he calmly stated.

I knew that right outside in the courtroom was a room full of press. Full of my family. How could I admit that I was a failure? A loser. A junkie. How would I deal with the crippling shame that was my reality? What I didn't realize then, but that I do now, is that this was the same toxic shame that had been my reality since I was a very little girl. The only difference was the circumstances.

The prosecutor wanted me in prison, but thankfully, the judge took a different approach.

For the first time in years, I was finally getting honest.

"I need help," I told Judge Peter Espinoza. "I'm dying. I can go to prison and just keep being a horrible person, but I want to get better. I am done ruining my life."

Judge Espinoza gave me a chance to save my life. I was sentenced to one year of treatment.

My mom and Mike had already reached out to a rehab center that was willing to take me on a scholarship, and it was arranged by the court that the center would pick me up two days later.

I was released into the custody of one of the techs from the facility, an older white guy who came and got me in a big, ugly van. I was sketched out until I asked him if we could get cigarettes.

He smiled, perhaps the first kind smile I had seen in weeks, "We can do better than that." He took me through the drive through of McDonald's. I had barely eaten in two weeks and was still reeling from the horrors of my detox.

"I know," he told me as we ate cheeseburgers in the McDonald's parking lot. "I've been where you are, Alexis. It's up to you. But you don't ever have to go back."

I don't know why, but I believed him.

That is the miracle of recovery. We meet a stranger, and because they too have eaten McDonald's after kicking heroin in jail for two weeks, because they too have lost all hope, because they too have stopped being able to look at themselves in the mirror, we believe them when they say it will get better.

I ate that cheeseburger and I smoked that cigarette and it was the best meal of my life. It was the first day of the rest of my life.

## Chapter Thirteen

# Growing Up for Real

*"To be fully alive, fully human, and completely awake*
*is to be continually thrown out of the nest.*
*To live fully is to be always in no-man's-land, to*
*experience each moment as completely new and fresh.*
*To live is to be willing to die over and over again."*
*—Pema Chodron*

You would think, after being a drug addict for years, I would have understood how rehab worked. But I had never been to one; and nobody in my family had ever been to one, either. I was clueless; I just knew you had to be really fucked up to end up here. And I was fucked up. But that didn't automatically mean I was going to take it seriously, not at first.

Thankfully, there were also lots of boys in rehab— and just the kind I liked…damaged, dangerous and addicted.

I would show up to the group meetings and therapy appointments, but I was just going through the motions. Here is what I realized, and what we help people to realize at Alo House, the recovery center my husband and I run: rehab is a window. It's a small glimpse into the outside world. For 30 days or 60 days or whatever, you get to see what life looks like sober. You start to taste food again. You begin to laugh. You hopefully get what Gabor Maté—invoking the Catholic monk and mystic, Thomas Merton—calls "a little taste of victory."

I don't think I saw victory at first, but I heard laughter. And when you spend years living in darkness and misery, laughter is the brightest light in the world. It opens up your soul, and if that's something you've been avoiding, it gives you the courage to look. I wasn't yet ready to dance with my soul, but I was ready to start dancing with other people. Their laughter made me feel alive again. Alive in ways I had never really been.

Still, if you don't start doing the work, the window will once again begin to close. Because the laughter will get you into the work, but it's the work that gets you out of rehab. That work isn't easy when all you know is misery. I'd never had the chance to be carefree. I was always carrying the worries, burdens and responsibilities of my parents. I was taught how to be cool and keep everything inside.

I had to learn again how to be a kid and let it out.

I also needed to learn how to behave.

Basically, I grew up without rules. When my mom grounded me, I always got out of it within an hour or so. I was allowed to smoke pot in the house at the age of 14. When I decided I didn't want to go to school anymore, that was fine, my mom just set me up to be homeschooled. I had lived a life without consequences until I found myself vomiting in that jail cell.

Rehab was all about consequences for me: I got into trouble for everything. It was about growing up and learning how to be a productive member of society, which means being held accountable.

Didn't want to go the second AA meeting of the day? *Too bad!* I have to make my bed? *Sure do!*

I probably hadn't made my bed at home in 13 years. And I barely had a closet; I just had piles of clothes on the floor, with a trail that I made to walk through them.

I was defiant and obnoxious in those early days. I am so beyond grateful to everyone who had patience with me. Instead of focusing on recovery (because really, what was I going to do with all that pain?) I focused on boys. And when you don't have drugs, trust me, boys are the next best things. I knew escape like the back of my hand. I was being asked to feel, and all I wanted to do was numb. Since I didn't have any drugs, and still had enough faith to believe I might not need them, I used distraction to get by. The problem with distraction is that no one heals there. They just postpone the work. It's like living in purgatory, without your medicine, but without anything comparable to replace it with.

I had this awesome chance to fix things, this incredible gift. Instead I shut down, waiting for it to be over.

Here's the fucked up thing about spiritual awakenings. They don't happen when the sun is shining and the sky is full of rainbows and unicorns. They happen when you're terrified to get out of bed. When you don't remember who you are and don't know where to go. They happen when you're not sure you can breathe through the moment. When you think you might just want to stop breathing altogether.

I was two months into rehab when I relapsed. A group of the kids were doing whippets, which is basically laughing gas, or nitrous oxide. Inhaling enough can make you feel like your brain is shutting down, which for many of us, is a welcome relief. You can get high on nitrous by sucking on a canister of whipped cream, at the cost of how many brain cells I can only guess. Since nitrous doesn't show up on a drug screen, some of the other clients had bought some at the grocery store and pulled it out as we were driving to therapy.

There I was in the back of a car, just off the Venice Boardwalk, doing whippets. Within a minute of my high wearing off, I found myself hitting a new kind of bottom. It was an emotional one, although it happened to take the form of a mounted policeman who came up on our car.

It was my bright idea to tell him we were just sucking on helium to make our voices funny. Somehow he believed me. I avoided going to prison for violating the terms of my parole.

A huge realization came from an act as stupid as sucking on a whipping cream canister. In rehab, I was safe and cared for the first time in a long time, but emotionally, I was a fucking wreck.

There I was, faced with the truth that this was a mess I created, and it was one I needed to clean up.

My window briefly opened again.

It was a stupid escape, a stupid high, but when we emerged from it, heading back to therapy, it all hit me at once. I didn't want to escape anymore. I wanted to grow up. And not in the way I was forced to as a kid. I didn't want to be responsible for other people's lives or mistakes. I just wanted to be responsible for mine. I wanted to be able to raise my hand and say, "I'm Alexis, and I'm an alcoholic." "I'm Alexis, and I'm an addict." "I'm Alexis, and I fucked up." Believe it or not, there was something so empowering about these words. In one breath, you can admit the truth and gain entry into a club that I am profoundly proud to belong to today. Not just of AA (though that one is great, too). But to a tribe of others who have struggled, who have rightly done what they had to do at the time, and who after having enough, made a vow to wake up and take responsibility for their lives. I went to a meeting the next day, and that's exactly what I did. I started to really wake up.

I felt the one thing that had been missing since I showed up to treatment: humility. I finally surrendered.

I didn't want to go to prison for whippets. I didn't want to fuck my whole life up; I wanted to actually live. Because that laughter had done something to me, it gave me a glimpse of hope. And just like that first high from dope, I wanted to chase it. I nearly killed myself so many times over, and none of those big dramatic experiences woke me up, but that stupid hit of nitrous on March 8, 2011 rang that bell for me. It wasn't a bang, but a whisper. And I heard it loud and clear.

That was the last time I ever used.

I wish I could tell you that "Here Comes the Sun" started playing, and all my pain disappeared. But I don't think it looks like that for any of us. I had been using drugs since the age of 14 and now I was being asked to get up every day and get through it sober. That was a hard ask. It was brutal some days. I didn't know how to look at myself in the mirror. I knew I didn't want to be the girl detoxing in jail, but I didn't know how to love the woman I was becoming either. She was trapped between being the adult she had always been asked to be, but failed at, and the child she never got to be.

But something happened: I was freer than before.

It was like being 13 years old again, when I first started using, except only now I was on the verge of turning 20. I had no idea who I was or what I was supposed to do. It seemed like everyone around me knew that I was just barely keeping my head above water.

I'm sure to everyone else, it looked like I was just trying to be some loud, cocky tough girl, but that's what you do when you're a terrified little girl: you put on the biggest armor you can find. But I slowly started to allow myself to be open and vulnerable to the process that has been guiding my life ever since. There was a man at the meeting I went to every day, and I asked him if he knew a woman who might sponsor me. He gave me the number for a woman who I still call to this day. Debra is both a spiritual advisor and trusted friend, and she generously and gently helped me through my metamorphosis.

I honestly don't know if I would be here right now if not for Debra. She led me through peeling those first layers of the onion. Except my onion was made of metal and was covered in spikes. But she ignored my bravado. She patiently loved me in spite of myself; she offered me true compassion. And because of that acceptance, I started opening up in ways that I never had before.

I started meeting me in the process.

And that man who gave me her number? I ended up marrying him.

Evan jokes that he didn't have a lot of hope for me. I would come in and share things like, "Oh my God, I just got voted the best celebrity mugshot on TMZ." (Imagine me saying that in the blasé vocal fry for which we Valley girls are so famous.) He laughed to himself before going home and Googling me, which was probably my goal. Plus, there was part of me still clinging to my former identity.

He claims he saw something there, a faint glimmer of something more. Evan didn't see me again for almost a year. He says he was absolutely shocked by the woman I turned into during that time. To this day, he credits my transformation as the reason he refuses to give up on any addict trying to get clean.

After my first year in treatment, my mom was still trying to be my "momager," determined that I could reinvent my career, and hers by extension.

"You should get back out there," my mom suggested. But I knew that back "out there" was a dangerous place for me.

While in rehab I went back to school to become a drug and alcohol counselor, starting the two-year certification program. After I got out, I found a job working at another rehabilitation facility as an intern. Now I was the one telling people to get up and go to group. I was enforcing rules. I was the one driving the big old van.

Evan and his group of friends sort of overlapped with some of my friends, and we started seeing each other a lot at meetings. Evan was from Canada and just opening up his first sober living with a couple of his friends. He had five years of sobriety and seemed absolutely committed to his recovery.

Every time he shared, I felt like my armor was being pierced a little.

When I was about a year sober, Evan and I started to date.

Authenticity means accepting yourself in all that you do. It means not shying from your mistakes or living in the denial of the past. It also means accepting the best parts of yourself—and that can be even harder work. Authenticity asks that we get rid of the layers of shame, fear and self-limiting beliefs. That we fall in love with our own hearts.

Today, I am a 28-year old mom, living in the suburbs, covered in tattoos. I'm still working on finding my tribe out here. It isn't easy in these kinds of more conservative circles, but I won't trade me for anything. About six months into sobriety, I began to walk the road that led me to where I am now. I began to find the self-love to finally replace the self-loathing. I used to be so consumed with what people thought about me, and it made me a fucking mess.

Now, I am a practicing Buddhist who loves Jesus—the real Jesus. The brown skinned Jew, who was a refugee from Nazareth and who led a radical, heretical movement to democratize our access to God. I love the radical social activist who fought for the sick, the poor and the broken. The man who said, "He that is without sin among you, let him first cast a stone at her."

Who said, "You are gods; you are all sons of the Most High."

When you finally let go of what other people think of you, you get to be you. For so long, I had only been able to rely on myself to survive. But now, I have discovered that the Universe is so much bigger than that. It is bigger than all our fears, all our worst moments; all those windows of opportunity that we worry are closing for good. Because at any given moment, we can decide to reach out and do it differently. At any moment, we can choose life. We can also reach out and choose love.

We just have to be willing to look at ourselves in the mirror and hold our own gaze.

## Chapter Fourteen

# Love Heals

*"Love is not something we give or get;*
*it is something that we nurture and grow,*
*a connection that can only be cultivated between*
*two people when it exists within each one of them —*
*we can only love others as much as we love ourselves."*
*—Brené Brown*

My whole life I had been taught that men were a means to something else: money, drugs, self-confidence and identity. I was never single. But I was also never really in love. I mean, I loved my boyfriends, but it was always so hard to separate where need ended and love began.

How can you love someone when you have no fucking clue how to love yourself? How can you have the strength to see them clearly for who they are? How can you have the courage to not look away? I was taught how to be obsessed and selfish and vain, but nothing about love. Because love required that I look outside myself to know and understand some-one else.

I never had the chance to figure out who I was because I was always taking care of someone else, whether that was my mom, Gabby or Tess. I would swing from giving all of me away to not giving any-thing at all. I had no idea that love lived in the balance.

The first time Evan asked me out, he suggested coffee after the Malibu meeting. It had been months since we had seen each other.

I still had such a long road ahead of me, but it was clear that if I were willing to do the deal, I would begin to heal. But like I said, that didn't mean I was single. They say in AA that you shouldn't date anyone for your first year sober, so of course, I did. I was da-ting some guy who I really didn't care about, just because he was there, and I still needed a distraction. I said yes to Evan's invite, and that night, broke up with the other guy. Because though I had no idea where our coffee date would lead, I knew this: Evan was exactly the kind of man I wanted to be with, be-cause he was the kind of person I wanted to be.

He was smart and funny and had something I'd never realized was so important: kindness. People met him and they instantly respected him. They trusted him because he cared about other people. They say in the program to surround yourself with the people who have what you want. I wanted what Evan had. I wanted people to respect me. But most importantly, I wanted them to trust me because I could be trusted.

I wanted to be kind.

It didn't take long into our first date for me to realize that I wanted more than Evan's integrity. If you can fall in love on a first date, it was happening. After the second date, we sat on the beach after having dinner together, talking about our childhoods. They were both full of chaos, mental health problems and addiction. Both of us had been stressed out little kids, raised in very unsafe environments.

"I guess there just comes a point," Evan told me as we stared out at the ocean, "where you just want to break the pattern. Where you want to do things different than your parents, you know, and break the curse."

They were the words I had been waiting my whole life to hear.

I wanted a do-over, and though I didn't think I would be building my own family any time soon—oh, how God laughs—I knew that I wanted to break the cycle of intergenerational trauma. I wanted to build a family on love, trust, respect and tradition. By the time Evan dropped me off at my apartment, I couldn't imagine my life without him.

I was 20 and newly sober. I had been in jail just a year before. There was so much about my life that was still shattered and on the floor, but I had already been adulting for so long, I didn't need another 10 years to grow up. I had been a grown up since the age of 10.

What I needed to do was turn that sacrificed childhood into something worth growing up for.

The universe gives us all these spiritual tools to survive our trauma, and we can either ignore them or see what kind of lives we can actually build with them. What did our hardest times teach us? And how can we use those lessons to build better lives? How can we find our superpowers amongst the survival skills? Because it's those powers, which not only help us to heal, but maybe most importantly, help us to offer healing to others.

My superpower was being mature beyond my age, and now, it was time for me to show up for it.

Evan was that opportunity. I loved that he wasn't in the entertainment industry—a miracle in LA—and he didn't seem to care at all about my past, either the celebrity part or the prison part (he still has never watched a full episode of *Pretty Wild*).

"I'm interested in who you are now," he told me, and by accepting me, truly allowed me the freedom to be who I was. After our second date, he asked to meet my mom, which felt a little crazy, but I also knew that he was 35, and as he explained, he was, "done fucking around."

"My mom is insane," I warned him.

"That's okay," he replied. "So was mine."

I think it was our mothers that actually brought us together. Like my own mother, Evan's was sometimes incredibly loving and hilarious, creative and adventurous, and other times, she just couldn't keep it together, putting him in very unsafe situations. Evan's mom battled bipolar disorder. When he was 14, she decided she couldn't fight it anymore, and took her life. Because of his upbringing, Evan also had to do too much of his own parenting. So I think when we met each other, it just felt like, we don't have to do this alone anymore; we can do this together.

But Evan was still a guy, and after rushing head-long into the relationship, he freaked out. The night he came over and met my mom, he dropped me off at my apartment without coming in.

"Are you sure you don't want to hang out at all?" I asked, my stomach sinking.

"No, I've got to get to this work thing," he lied.

A few hours later, he called me and said he felt like we were going too fast, and that he needed a break. I've had a lot of bad shit happen to me, but that was one of the worst moments of my life. I knew with everything in me that we were supposed to be to-gether, and while we're not always right when we feel that way, sometimes we are.

Before we hung up, I got as honest with him as I had ever been: "That's fine, we can stop dating, but I just need to say this, I think I've fallen in love with you."

And then I hung up.

The problem was, we kept seeing each other at meetings. One night, right around Halloween, I had plans to meet up with some other guy, and so I was dressed up as a super sexy Freddy Krueger at the meeting. Evan and I ran into each other, and it nearly broke my heart all over again. I cancelled my date and went home in tears. I loved him so much, and though I was only 20, I was done getting dressed up super sexy, hoping to meet a guy.

I didn't want to do that shit.

I wanted to break the cycle of intergenerational trauma. And I wanted to do that with Evan. I guess I wasn't alone. Because two weeks later, Evan called me and apologized. He asked if we could try again, and I agreed.

"But don't pull that shit again," I warned him.

A few weeks later, we moved in together.

Since getting sober, my relationship with my mom had only become more toxic. Though my mom supported my sobriety, it felt like the healthier I got, the more she clung to this old idea of me. In family systems, they call me the "Identified Patient" (IP). All of the family's disorders and problems get put on the IP, and then when the IP gets well, it can create a very difficult dynamic. The other members of the family are forced to look at themselves, maybe for the first time in a long time.

One of the hardest things to surrender is what other people think of us, especially those that think they know us best. Our parents and family have one version of us, but usually that identity is who they *want* us to be, not who we really are. As we get healthier, they try to force us back into the old role. In order to get healthy, we have to remember that they don't really know us. They don't know how powerful we truly are, and how powerful we've become.

My mom felt like I was giving up opportunities by not committing to my modeling and acting career. She felt like the burglaries actually gave me an opportunity to capitalize on the infamy, but I was hiding out in the recovery world, refusing to make public appearances. But I knew that my sobriety had to come first. If I went back to the clubs and the late nights and my relationship with Tess, I was doomed.

Evan gave me another option. I moved in with him and his roommates and started my internship at a rehab while I got my drug and alcohol counseling certification. Because Evan was Canadian, he had to go back home to renew his visa soon after I moved in. The problem was, once he landed in Canada, his visa was denied and they wouldn't let him back into the States. He was stuck there. I was living in his apartment with all his roommates, and because I had a felony, I couldn't fly to Canada to go see him. And he couldn't fly back to LA.

It was crazy. We went from being on a break to now being kept apart. I was so upset, but as his lawyer explained, there was no work-around.

Finally, one night on the phone, four months after he left, Evan proposed the only solution that made sense: "Will you marry me?"

I didn't even hesitate. "Of course I will!"

Here's how I knew it was the real deal: in every previous relationship, I'd relied heavily on the intoxicating effects of oxytocin and novelty, the high of having fun with a new person.

But with Evan, I couldn't do that. We weren't able to have romantic dates because we were so far apart. Instead, I was having the opportunity to fall deeper and deeper in love with a man who was thousands of miles away. We would talk for hours, like that night on the beach.

I didn't need physical intimacy to feel this. It was real love.

Six weeks later, we met up in Mexico and got married. It was just the two of us, a few friends, Gabby and our parents. And it was the most perfect wedding I could have ever imagined. Our good friends Robert and Ian played "Here Comes the Sun" as I walked down the aisle.

Tess was there too, causing just the right amount of chaos.

During this time, my mom was on a new mission—to clear my name and prove once and for all that I had been falsely accused of being part of the "Bling Ring." She had files and photos, everything but the wall with the red yarn connecting it all together.

Evan, always so wonderful, told me that he hoped my mom *wouldn't* clear my name. That it was my truth and my story to own. He told me that my story would help me to better help others. It sure didn't feel like that, but in those dark days, sometimes his optimism was my only light.

We were again alone on the beach, only about nine months after that second date.

Evan told me, "You know this isn't just so I can get back in the States? This is for forever, okay?"

The waves crashed in front of us, as I leaned into him and said, "I know."

We wanted to do this life together, and US Customs and Immigration wasn't going to stop us.

Unfortunately, being married didn't give him the immediate ability to cross the border. After we exchanged vows, he headed back to Canada to work out the details of emigrating while I returned to LA. I got us our own little apartment and started setting it up, waiting for him to come home, unsure of when, exactly, that was going to be.

Then one day, he called me, "Babe, I'm on my way."

I screamed with joy. Finally, after months away, and one quickie Mexican wedding, we were going to be back together. Evan came home and went back to work opening up his first sober living. I was finishing up the hours for my certification, and it felt like we were finally building a life for ourselves.

And then that life got bigger: I found out I was pregnant.

It wasn't my first time getting pregnant, but it was the first time I knew this baby was meant to be.

"Are you sure?" Evan asked, and I swore I could see hope in his eyes.

We were married three months when I became pregnant with Harper. It was scary, and we both knew it was a huge leap, but this was the promise we talked about on that magical night, sitting on the beach. We were going to break the curse.

Unfortunately, my mom was doing everything she could to pull me back.

Toxic relationships are like their own drug. The people involved go through their own cravings and withdrawals and my mom wanted our old relationship back, with me as the scapegoat. Without me there, she was being asked to look at herself in the mirror, and she didn't want to see it. She wanted to focus on me; she wanted to escape through me. But I wasn't going to be her drug anymore.

The producers for the movie, *Bling Ring,* reached out, and wanted to talk about my story. Sofia Coppola was at the helm.

"You need to write a book," my mom demanded. She told me she was going to be my manager again. I would give her the customary 15 percent, despite the fact that she had no industry relationships and no real experience packaging and selling projects.

Sadly, she only saw dollar signs.

But I was becoming very pregnant, and just wanted to have my baby and be with my husband. Plus, beginning at about the two-month mark, I bled throughout my entire pregnancy. Every day that I kept my baby felt like a miracle. Getting out and selling books and projects and appearances just felt dangerous. I had finally found safety with Evan. And my mom was threatening to blow it up.

I lost my job at the treatment center because of all my medical issues with the pregnancy, and Evan still wasn't making any money with the sober living. We were living off my severance, plus a small life rights payment that Sofia had given me. I had so much financial insecurity, but however tempting it was, I knew what my mom was asking of me was wrong.

"You've got to stop this," Evan finally demanded. "Your mom is not an agent or a manager. You need her to be your mom right now. This is not good for you and the baby."

Evan stood up for me, putting my health and well being first. Something no one had ever done for me. And through his strength, I began to build my own. I didn't know how to stand up to my mom, but I knew how to model Evan's behaviors. I watched him set boundaries, and I wanted to create that sanctuary for myself.

We all have the opportunity to divorce our parents—and not in a way that is cold or mean. But in the way that we don't have to play the old roles anymore. We can reset the contract that we signed long before we were born, when we absorbed their fears and their traumas. We can demand that we be treated in ways that align with who we are today, right now, in this ever-powerful moment. And we can leave the old patterns behind. We can choose what kind of daughter or son we want to be, even if we can't choose what parents we got.

I called my mom and told her that I didn't want her to be my manager on the book, or on anything else, and that I needed to take care of myself.

"You've always been a selfish bitch!" she screamed at me.

"I'm the selfish bitch?" I screamed back. In that moment, I had a revelation. I had always seen my mom as the victim and my father as the perpetrator, but now I began to see how my mom had been abusing me my whole life. The hardest part was having to question whether she even loved me at all. Or whether she, my own mother, was just using me.

She didn't realize that by trying to clear my name in the *Bling Ring*, she was really only trying to clear her own name. If I were innocent, which I wasn't, then she would somehow be let off the hook *as a parent*. All her "proof" didn't matter. I didn't want my name cleared. I just wanted to move forward with my life. And she should have known better. My mom has taken enough self-help courses to fill an entire room with handouts and binders. Even with all that, she still couldn't see the truth of what's important in life.

But I was pregnant, and I wasn't having it. I already wanted to protect my baby. I wanted to keep her safe from toxic families. I wanted to make sure she was never abused or exploited or forced to question her mother's love.

After our fight on the telephone, my mom found correspondence between myself and the relative who molested me where we had been cordial, as many victims and perpetrators are. My mom told other family members about this, figuring it was a "gotcha" moment, and accused me of lying to them about the sexual abuse.

Here I am, in the third trimester of an already very difficult pregnancy, just trying to keep our home afloat after being fired from my job. Instead of being supportive, my mom is questioning whether I was really abused in attempt to pit our family against me. I'm not sure how she thought this would land her back in the "momager" role, or if maybe was just purely in the name of punishment. It was horrible, whatever it was.

So bad in fact that my super spiritual sponsor, who was always so level-headed, called my mom, and asked, "Do you even realize what you're doing?"

And for once, my mom stopped. But more importantly, for the first time, I was able to feel a sense that other people had my back, finally.

I so rarely had anyone stand up and protect me. But over time, with the love and support of others, that thick armor that I walked into recovery with began to fall away. I began to feel safe enough in Evan's love to become vulnerable. Not just with him, but with other friends from the program and people I worked with. I started to become more vulnerable with myself.

Though we were going through a horrible, scary time, we also had a baby on the way. It only brought Evan and I closer together in ways I'm not sure we would have been able to do on our own. Our loyalty to each other became our superpower. It was the foundation of the new relationship we were building, and the family we were about to begin. My mother didn't know what to do in the face of this new power of mine. She wanted to be part of our lives, although she seemed indifferent about being a grandmother.

She began to realize that I wasn't the same Alexis she had raised.

Every day, I was becoming stronger. I was becoming kind and loyal. I was becoming trustworthy. I was becoming a woman of integrity.

And I wasn't going to be treated like shit anymore.

## Chapter Fifteen

------------------------------------------------------------

# Birthing Life

*"There really are places in the heart you don't*
*even know exist until you love a child."*
*—Anne Lamott*

Giving birth is one of the most miraculous experiences on the planet. It feels like the most primal expression of being human, bringing a new life into this world. But even more than that, it is the biggest collision of fear and faith anyone can ever experience. It is the place where everything you hope will be—a new life, the realization of a dream—meets every fear you can have—your own survival, and more importantly, that of your baby. And at a certain point, there's very little you can do to stop the process.

Every mother has her own unique birthing experience, but with my first baby, I was determined to make it as natural and nurturing as possible. My body had already been so damaged throughout the years; I didn't want any more physical trauma. I didn't want a room full of people poking and examining me while I was in the most vulnerable state a woman could be in. I just wanted the quiet calm of giving birth at home. But what I discovered was that giving birth is a lot like raising a child, and like life itself for that matter. Nothing ever goes as planned.

I started working with a midwife, as Evan and I prepared to have a water birth. My water broke around 4 am one morning, and our midwife rushed over. The contractions started, and my labor began to progress quickly. But despite pushing for hours and hours, the baby wasn't passing through the canal. My midwife did another check, and realized that Harper was Frank breech, folded in half, with her butt pushing through first. The midwife stated calmly that we needed to go to the hospital. Now. Evan jumped out of the tub and quickly got dressed as I threw on a robe.

We raced to the hospital in our little Toyota, weaving in and out of rush hour traffic. I sat in the back, pushing myself up with my feet so that my butt hovered a few inches off the seat for the entire drive, since Harper was already starting to slip out of me. Every few seconds, Evan would check on me in the rear view mirror. He later confided he thought there was a good chance both the baby and I were going to die. He just kept driving though.

The midwife, following in her car behind us, called ahead to the hospital so when we arrived, they were waiting for me with a wheelchair at the drop-off curb.

They raced me down the hall of the hospital, as I cried out, over and over, "Help me! Somebody help me!"

I was standing up on the footrests as my baby was starting to come out of me, not noticing or caring that my robe was wide open. I was terrified and no one around me looked any more reassured. Evan watched the faces of nurses and doctors blanch with horror as we were whisked past them on the way to the birth unit.

There is no lonelier place on earth than when you think something might be wrong with your baby. I looked over to Evan and could see the concerned expression on his face.

I pleaded to him, even between my screams, "Are we going to lose her?"

His face was made of stone, "No, we're not."

The doctor, who had been giving a talk to the kids at a local school, was called in to perform an emergency C-section. It seemed to take forever to prep me. They couldn't do anything for my pain until they were ready to make the first incision, so that 20-minute wait was maybe the most unbearable of my life. At that point, they could have removed both my legs to get her out, and I wouldn't have cared. I just wanted to see her breathe.

When they finally wheeled me into the operating room, the midwife, who had been our only source of comfort and guidance up until this point, broke down crying to Evan. She said she was so sorry she hadn't realized that the baby was breech. Evan, even in his fog of fear and panic, and more than a little resentment, forgave her.

They brought Evan into the operating room to be there when they delivered the baby. He was on the side of the little curtain. I guess Harper was already wedged so far down my birth canal, that in order to bring her out of my stomach, they had to yank on her. My whole body was heaving up and down as they struggled to pull her back up and out. It was horrible and traumatic and everything that I didn't want, and still, when they put that crying baby on my chest, I sobbed. She was alive. She was beautiful. And she was all I ever wanted.

The day Harper was born wasn't just one of the greatest days of my life, it was also one of the biggest lessons I have ever learned. Because when I first held her, an emotion flooded my consciousness that I never knew existed: the desire to protect someone with every cell in my being. I wanted to give her the one thing that both my parents failed to give me—*safety*.

The next few days were a blur. I know at some point in the heat of the action, I had Evan run out to call my probation officer. I had to let her know we unexpectedly left Los Angeles County to get to the hospital in Ventura County.

There was no way I was going to run afoul of the Los Angeles Superior Court again.

I finally got out of the hospital, and we took our little baby girl home to our apartment. Those were some of the sweetest memories of my life. We didn't even know what time it was, days would blend with nights, punctuated only by the odd visits of friends and family coming to meet Harper. Our time was spent resting, nursing and cooking meals, TV on in the background, and the baby slept through all of it.

Our domestic bliss was interrupted by the release of the *Bling Ring* movie. And my mom was back at it again. She is like the *Terminator* of fame. She was talking to the *LA Times* and trying to get me to do interviews.

"This is your moment!" she encouraged me one afternoon, as I breastfed my newborn baby, still healing from my C-section. I just shook my head.

The media found out where we were living, and with the movie out, there was renewed interest in my life. I was sixty pounds overweight, struggling with PTSD from Harper's birth experience and feeling the onset of post-partum depression. One day, they took a photo of me where I looked particularly exhausted— you know, because I had a fucking newborn. I had no idea they took it and happened to see the photo online a few days later. The comments section was brutal.

They always say, don't read the comments! I wish I could say I was enlightened enough that the insults didn't hurt. I have tried to view the mean comments as the price I pay for being vulnerable and putting myself out there, but they can still trigger that shame reflex and make me sad sometimes. In these instances, I know that my only job is to dig deep into my compassion, and to think about the people who are so hurt that they don't have any other way to express their trauma than to target strangers with projections of their own pain. I can only wonder what must have happened to them that they hurt so badly.

In my fragile state, I read the hateful comments and fell apart. I started getting really fearful of people hurting us. To this day, I still have a really bad phobia around locking my doors and windows, afraid someone is going to break into my house and hurt me and my babies. And yes, I'm very aware of the karmic overtones of this particular form of OCD.

My mom and stepdad, Jerry, offered Evan, Harper, and I the choice to move in with them. They lived in a gated townhouse community where we would be more protected. After struggling with the idea of moving in with my parents, for obvious reasons, Evan eventually capitulated. Evan was still getting the business up, and though he was finally beginning to make a small income, we were struggling. But mostly, he just knew that this was something I wanted, and he wanted me to feel safe.

So there I was, locked into this conflict with my mom over not sufficiently pursuing my fame, struggling with postpartum depression, trying to figure out how to be a new mom. Now I was about to move from the frying pan into the fire. As the movie came out, my mom's bid to clear my name hit a crescendo. She was deep into an investigation into the lead detective on the case, who allegedly had done shady things, including supposedly sending suggestive texts to witnesses. We also discovered that he had participated in the production of the movie. My mom saw an opportunity to overturn the plea deal.

"We need to get you back with an attorney," she argued. "A good attorney."

But I didn't want to fight. I served my time. It was over.

She was driving a lot of people crazy with this manic, selfish quest for my vindication, including my stepdad, Jerry. He had been living with this particular version of my mom—we'll call her Detective Andrea—for over a year at this point. So two days later after Evan and I moved in with them, Jerry moved out. He left my mom after nearly 13 years together.

My mom lost her mind, obviously. And now Evan and I were stuck.

Just like with drugs, toxic relationships have to hit a bottom. We have to walk through the dark night of the relationship's soul, right up to the breaking point, where we either do it differently, or we quit it entirely. We have to be willing to walk away. Because in that moment, when we're willing to surrender the relationship, we open the door for healing. We release our grip on what we think the it should be, and we give each other the chance to turn it into the relationship it can become.

I can look back on that time and wish it never happened, but I'm not sure my mom and I would have healed our relationship any other way. And after everything, I was glad to help her through what was a very difficult time in her life, one that I think we're still recovering from. But we wouldn't have been able to begin that healing without Evan.

A few months after Harper was born, *Vice* magazine reached out and asked if I would write a column about addiction and recovery for them. I always loved writing, and now I would have a fun, creative platform where I could express myself. Better yet, instead of people writing about me, I would be the author of my own story. One of the first pieces I published was on millennials and our relationship with our parents, and in it, I talked about my own mother's and mine.

She read it one night as we were going to bed and started in with me about it.

I closed the door to our room right as I heard her holler at me, "I know Evan had something to do with this!"

The next morning, just as the sun was coming up, Evan was downstairs, alone, having his coffee and reading the news, something he has always loved to do. It's his quiet time. My mom came downstairs to get something and couldn't pass up the opportunity to confront him.

"Alexis cannot be writing about me publicly like that," she firmly declared.

Evan, barely looking up from his coffee, calmly stated that this was my story, and that I could tell it to whomever I wanted.

She leaned toward him, and angrily complained, "Do you know what this could do to me? I have a reputation to maintain!"

My husband is an extremely calm man, no matter what is going on in his internal world. And his patience and tolerance could probably be confused with pacifism if you don't know about his breaking point. My mom was about to find out about his breaking point.

Evan put down his coffee and looked up from his phone, literally laughing out loud, "Ha! Do you know what your reputation is?" He told her everything I ever wanted to say but was too afraid, and an absolute miracle happened. My mother listened.

She was stunned.

Evan was just trying to get back to reading the news, and to of course defend his wife's right to be who she was and freely tell her own story. In one short year, he already watched my mom try to profit off my name and my pain a few times, and he'd seen enough.

That morning, I think my mom saw the same thing in Evan that I saw. He didn't want anything from me. He just wanted to be my partner.

As my mom said later, it was the best thing that ever happened to her. She said that, in that moment, she saw the chaos she was living in, and her part in creating it. And here was this new baby, this new life, and she had the chance to turn hers around. After that day, she quit smoking pot, and she quit drinking so much. But more importantly, she started acting better towards all of us. Evan and I ended up living with her for another six months. In that time, she and I actually began to build a real relationship.

Not as mother and child, where neither of us knew who was who, but as two grown women. It wasn't perfect, it's still not perfect, but it was wildly, unimaginably better.

Healing old relationships is like giving birth to a new life. You have to go through the dark canal and hope that you both survive the process. It's scary to say that you don't know if you can keep loving someone you love with all your heart. You have to let faith and fear collide and know that if you can stay present, if you can breathe through it, you'll create something new and precious in place of what was before. You'll get to start over. And there is no greater miracle than pressing the reset button and getting to work to get it right the next time.

Right after Harper turned one, Evan and I moved out into our own place in Studio City. We decided we wanted to have another baby. Then, as quickly as we got pregnant with Harper, we found ourselves struggling on our second. I had a miscarriage. At the time, I didn't have the coping skills that I needed to get through it. I couldn't see the big picture of what was happening. I was taking care of a baby, trying to figure out who I was in all of that, and still healing from mostly unprocessed pain. So much had happened in such a short period of time, I just became overwhelmed.

I started having panic attacks and everything felt like it was imploding.

Soon, I would have like 10 panic attacks a day. I had to stop driving. I could barely parent. On a number of occasions, I would have to call the ambulance for myself. There were days where I couldn't even get out of bed.

"Alexis," my mom sat by me while I lay in bed. "Honey, we need to figure this out."

Evan had called my mom because even he couldn't rouse me. I felt like I had been given all these gifts—my sobriety, my husband, my daughter—and now, I couldn't show up for them.

I went to a psychiatrist because I didn't know what else to do, and they started running me down a menu of anti-depressants. Unfortunately, that only made things worse. For some people, psychotropic medications might work great, but Zoloft, Prozac, Wellbutrin only made me feel worse, often with violent physical reactions. I almost put myself on a psych hold after starting the Prozac. I called Evan one day when he was at work, bawling, telling him that I thought I was going to kill myself, which obviously triggered his own childhood trauma around losing his mom to suicide. I didn't want to do that to him, or to Harper, and I finally decided I had to figure something out. I desperately needed to find something that would work.

I decided to dive into alternative healthcare.

I began to see a holistic doctor, an amazing woman named Dr. Sayana, who tested my blood for all kinds of things, and really took the time to study the different, and often alarming, results of those tests.

I started looking at my gut health. They say that 95 percent of our serotonin receptors are in our intestines, so intestinal health is directly related to our ability to manage, cope and react to life. Gut instincts aren't just a saying. They are scientific fact.

I had leaky gut and a lot of mold and heavy metals. I found out my adrenal functions were basically non-existent. Healthy levels of cortisol (the body's stress hormone) are necessary to get us up and out of bed and propel us throughout the day. I had exhausted my body's adrenal gland production from the prolonged exposures to stress that I had experienced since childhood. Now, without the calming effects of my "medicine." I started tackling all of these different ailments one at a time. I started creating space in the morning to build my peace with guided meditations. I started taking supplements to balance my system.

The word "balance" has begun to feel like an overused cliché. It's lost its meaning. For me, balance is acknowledging where I'm at right now. It's about accepting the feelings, not trying to control them. Balance is about creating a flow between my expectations and my abilities. And accepting when that flow feels more like a grind.

There are still days where I wake up and I don't want to get out bed. There are days where I can feel like fear is suffocating me, like I'm being trapped under a big wave. I can either fight it, and pretend everything is fine, or I can take the necessary steps to heal. Often, I just need be present and open to the experience. It always passes.

About a year after I began down the road of alternative healing, Evan and I got pregnant with our second child. At 10 weeks pregnant, my OB asked if I wanted to take this new blood test that they were offering. He showed me the brochure for it, and explained that it's to screen for genetic abnormalities, which given my age, wouldn't be a factor. We could also find out the baby's sex way before anyone could detect it in an ultrasound.

This sounded great, so we went for it.

The doctor explained that the lab would bill my insurance $5,000, but not to worry, that if it wasn't covered, that they would just charge us a cash rate of $100.

Then I got the call.

The results came back positive for Trisomy 13, which is a horrible and very rare chromosomal disorder. Of the babies born with Trisomy 13, or Patau Syndrome, 80 percent die within the first few hours or weeks outside of the womb. To say Evan and I were heartbroken doesn't even begin to describe how we felt. This was also happening during Christmastime. Evan's parents were in town from Canada and we were busy going to all these doctors' appointments. All the while I had a baby inside me who was going to be born just to die. Now neither of us could get out of bed.

The doctor said that they wanted to do another kind of testing and sent me to a geneticist. But as my OB warned, the initial blood test was 99.9 percent accurate. The results of the CVS test, which is performed by taking a sample of your placenta from up through your cervix, were no better. They also tested positive for Trisomy13. The genetic counselor told us to stay calm, though, and continue to the next test, which was an amniocentesis. This was an even more invasive procedure, where a six-inch needle was pressed through my stomach to remove a small amount of fluid from the amniotic sack that surrounds the fetus.

During all this testing, my OB told me, "I would strongly consider terminating the pregnancy. Let's get it on the calendar."

I was approaching 20 weeks at this point, and he said he wouldn't feel comfortable performing an abortion too far beyond that point. I told him about the testing, and that the genetic counselor told us to wait for the final results. I can perfectly remember the OB saying, rather coldly, "These things never end up going well."

But Evan and I decided to wait. I made the personal decision that, no matter what, I was going to carry the baby to term. These were the most difficult three months of my life. And somehow, like a miracle, I was sober for it. We thank God for the geneticist, Dr. John Williams at Cedars Sinai Hospital, and his genetic counselor for giving us the confidence to wait. We are so grateful that we didn't listen to that OB.

Because at 21 weeks, we got the test results from the amnio. Although the placenta was indeed positive, as the CVS test showed, our baby was negative for Trisomy13. She was completely, perfectly healthy. Our baby's placenta had different DNA than she did. According to one study, 25 percent of women who get the same positive blood test terminate their pregnancies without further testing. As we discovered during this whole thing, all our OB knew about the blood test,

"It's 99.9 percent effective!" he learned from the lab rep that sold it.

I changed OBs the next week.

Three months later, and after a terrible case of the mumps that saw me back at the hospital with a swollen face the size of a basketball, I gave birth to our miracle baby.

Dakota was absolutely perfect. I was able to have a vaginal birth after C-section (VBAC), delivering her naturally, just as I had wanted with Harper. Only about 10 percent of women opt for a VBAC, even though 90 percent of women are candidates. I was proud of myself. Evan saw me become a warrior priestess. I pulled her out myself, placed her on my chest, weeping with joy. Once again, we were alive.

Then, only a few days later, I started having chest pain. When Dakota was eight days old, we were doing her newborn photos and suddenly I felt like I couldn't breathe. I had shooting pains down my shoulder and back. I asked Evan to take me to the urgent care, and they wrote me a prescription for physical therapy.

I got back in the car and told Evan, "You need to take me to the emergency room now. Something's wrong."

I walked into the ER with Dakota strapped to me. They practically ripped the baby off and handed her to Evan, put the chest monitor on me, and rushed me into a room, while a doctor shouted for a CT scan. Evan stood there, stunned, holding Dakota.

"What's going on?" he asked. "Can someone tell me what's going on please?" But it seemed like no one would answer him, as they quickly prepped me. By that point, I felt like I could barely breathe. Every breath made me feel like I was being stabbed in the chest over and over.

As the doctor examined the scan, he nodded as though this was the result he expected, "You're having a pulmonary embolism."

I was about to die.

They immediately got an IV in me and started pumping me with blood thinners. I was freaking out because I had an eight-day old baby and a toddler who needed me. I was just beginning to breastfeed. How was Dakota going to eat? I was full of iodine contrast from the CT scan.

Motherhood has long been associated with martyrdom, but I know that my babies need me strong and healthy to live their own best lives. If I sacrifice everything for them, there will be nothing left of me. And yet, their safety always comes first. Their health and well-being and safe refuge in this world are my priorities. They always say to put your own oxygen mask on first, but I know how to hold my breath. My babies are still learning. It's a hard balance to strike.

I was 25 years old, and I wasn't sure if I was going to live to raise my children. It was the most terrifying day of my life. I ended up spending the next five days in the hospital, separated from my newborn Dakota and her big sister, Harper, who was only two at the time. My mom took Harper, and Evan somehow kept

Dakota going on the supply of frozen breast milk that I had already started storing away, not realizing how badly I would need it. We had to wait at least 24 hours before I could nurse her again. I cried every day, and yet I also knew that I would get through this. Like I said before, spiritual awakenings don't happen under rainbow skies.

They happen in the middle of the fucking hurricane.

I realized that I could either succumb to the grief, as I had been doing my whole life, or choose a different outcome. I wanted to be a warrior. I wanted to be the author of my own story and then I wanted to help other women to rewrite theirs. I saw that our lives could be so short, and that we could either spend them staring at ourselves in the mirror, waiting for the change, or we could go out and bring the change ourselves.

I also realized I wanted to help women bring life into the world.

I attended a friend's birth, and I was absolutely mesmerized by the miracle of watching a woman bring forth life. The fact that we build and create and nurture and produce life is just beyond fucking miraculous. We are so, so powerful. It's no wonder men have spent millennia trying to rob us of that power. I wanted to help women to connect into their own authority, to find out just how strong they could be. I started training to become a doula, and in the process, I began to connect into a side of womanhood I had never really known.

Motherhood is an unshakable bond. And in its trials and fears and challenges and victories, we find a fellowship of women. We might come from different places and different spaces. We might have different skin tones and sexual orientations. We might not agree on politics or religion or anything for that matter. But we have all stayed up through the night, holding a sick baby. We have all felt what it was like to hold a child to our chest and experience oneness with the divine. We have held our breaths as our children ride their bikes down the street or drive off into the night. We are bonded to each through our love, not just for each other, but for those little babies we will always hold in our hearts.

I began to see my role as a champion for women, whether they'd ever had a baby or not. I wanted to hold their hand and walk through that dark night with them and laugh with them on the other side. Because I might have grown up in pain, but I grew through love.

The marriage Evan and I started building that night on the beach became something bigger and better than we could have ever imagined. Don't get me wrong, it can still be hard. Neither of us is perfect. In fact, we can both be pretty fucked up sometimes, but just as we did at the beginning, we have each other's backs. We're a team. We can count on one another. We can trust each other. We keep each other safe. And we are raising our girls in safety. They don't need ever be scared that their parents won't be there to protect them. We will always make their needs and health and well-being a priority, especially when they can't do it on their own yet. For us, it's not just about honoring them as the little beings they are, it's about honoring the miracle that brought them to us in the first place.

The more I help other women with that miracle, the more I honor my own miraculous life—in all its good and bad and Bebe heels.

We neither regret the past, nor wish to shut the door on it. Instead, we embrace the superpowers that it brought us to healing, sometimes reluctantly, and we birth new life in the process. We heed the heroine's call to action. We walk through the obstacles. We begin again.

- - - - - - - - - - - - - - - - - - - - - - - - - - - - - - - - - - - - - - - - -

## Chapter Sixteen

# The Drama Stops Here

*"Don't turn away. Keep your gaze on the bandaged place.*
*That's where the light enters you."*
*–Rumi*

I wish I could say that when I got sober, all my relationships were magically healed. That my mom became a different woman overnight, or that I never get pissed off at my dad, who calls me like 10 times in a row just to tell me he loves me. He's obviously making up for lost time, and really doing his best at it, but it still drives me crazy sometimes.

And though my marriage is pretty damn amazing, I've also had to take a long hard look at how much I rely on my husband, and how I can start trusting myself more. But most of all, I have had to work on the most important relationship I have…the one with myself.

Because the only toxic relationship that I've ever really had is with myself. All those other relationships are just reflections of my own pain body that so badly needs to be healed. I can't think of a single toxic relationship that I willingly engaged in that wasn't serving me some real hard truths about an unhealed wound that I needed to tend to. Healing comes when you begin to accept those truths.

I have found a lot of magic comes from being sober, but the truth is, life can still be fucked up, and so can the people in it, including me. But here is the other side—the fucked up stuff is the fertile ground for our healing. It all becomes the raw materials we need to grow. Once we become our honest and authentic selves, shadow and all, people are forced to treat us differently than they did when we were hiding from ourselves. It's up to them if they really want to take a look at themselves, and we can only hope they do.

While writing for *Vice*, I had the honor of interviewing one of my personal heroes, Dr. Gabor Maté. Toward the end of the interview, he asked *me* a question, "Did you see the movie that was made about your life?"

I told him I hadn't, which is still true to this day.

"I'll tell you what I was struck by," he told me. "I was struck by Emma Watson's comment about your character—which wasn't about you, it was about the character that she was playing. She was actually hostile to the character. She had no compassion for the character that she was playing. Which was striking to me."

Emma Watson did an interview in *Rookie Magazine* and told Tavi Gevinson that she watched *Pretty Wild* so many times that it gave her anxiety. She wondered how anyone could watch it. Now I'm not going to tell a professional actor how to do her job, but as someone who is also a UN Women Goodwill Ambassador, Dr. Mate was right, she might have approached the role a little more sensitively. But I understand, it's hard to really look, and to have compassionate curiosity for others who are in pain. It's much easier to point fingers. "Tell them about the great work I do," my mom tells me when I sit down to interview her for this book. "You should do a chapter on it."

Here's the deal, my Mom does do great work. After that conversation with Evan, she finally really focused on her own deep soul-searching: who was she as a person? Who was she as a parent? How could she have done things better? How can she do things better now?

She started working with families who have addicted children. She helps them to get their kids into treatment, and then supports them during and after. But most importantly, she makes sure that these parents are doing the crucial, deep and sometimes painful work of looking at their own part in their children's addiction. Ironically, she's really good at it.

But she's still the kind of mom that wants me to write a chapter about it.

"Mom, it's my book!" I laugh, because though I am eight years sober, with two children myself, it's hard sometimes not revert to being a kid around your mom.

A big step towards maturity is sometimes having to accept that our parents are never going to change and learning to love and accept them exactly how they are. Both Evan and I are working on that, but we realize it's the little kids in us that still hold on to the idea that my mom and dad or his dad might become someone different. That they can just snap out of it. That they'll wake up one morning and say, "Great, no problem! I'll be the parent you always needed. First let me start by profoundly and irrevocably apologizing for everything I put you through, and for not protecting you." And though my mom has gotten so much better with reconciling herself with the past, and making up for it in so many ways, I've realized my happiness isn't dependent on her doing it just the way I need.

The same goes with my dad. I stopped counting his drinks years ago, and now today, I don't even feel like I need to. He really doesn't drink that way anymore anyway. He's grown up, too, and though he hasn't done the same amount of work as my mom, I can trust him in ways I never could as a child. I trust him with my own daughters, who he picks up from school on some days, and even watches sometimes. I could have never imagined that would be our future when I was 11 years old.

And yet, I've also had to accept that I am never going to get the apology from him that I need. So I can either continue to live in the trauma of that unhealed relationship or I can live my own life and be fully present and responsible. Once I started engaging my own healing, and my parents could no longer use me as their scapegoat, my role in the family changed. I've flown the nest.

I think parenting is also the great act of re-parenting. We each choose our partners out of woundedness or we choose them out of healing. I don't know how I lucked out and got the latter, but Evan and I parent through our healing together, and in that process, we get to make right what was done wrong, even if our parents still struggle.

But it isn't just our relationships with our parents that need to heal. For me, my relationships with Gabby, and especially Tess, had been as complicated and enmeshed as the relationships I had with my parents. I work with an amazing Reiki healer, Ute, who says that we have to decide the purpose of each relationship in our life, whether they are there for a reason, a season, or a lifetime. Sometimes we want that lifetime commitment, when maybe the Universe has a much more specific purpose for our love. I love Tess and her daughter so much, but I have also had to realize that we may never have the relationship I want. Our history might be too dark and too deep for us to ever heal together.

When we build a relationship on a lifetime's worth of unhealthy patterns, both parties need to be willing to dissect and address those old ways of being. And if you aren't able to unbraid the trauma bond, you might have to let it go. If you don't, you may be doomed to repeat it with someone else. Even recently, I found myself playing the same games and feeling the same feelings I always experienced with Tess. I would help and then feel hurt. And it's not Tess' or my fault. It's just the way we have always interacted with each other. The difference is that I am healthy enough today to know that I want it to change. I don't want to do it the old way anymore, because so much of my life is about healing and health and light.

The drama stops here.

A lot of people ask me about Gabby because she seemed so lost and innocent on the show. Like I said, Gabby's role in the family was the lost child. That spoke to some people. They wanted to make sure she was found. Over the last few years, Gabby has been working to find herself. Which is amazing for her but has also been hard for us. Because as much as I have been committed to my own growth and healing, it's still awkward when someone is going through their shit, and that shit is coming at you sideways. Gabby still has a lot of hurt and resentments directed at me, and I know that sometimes I haven't handled her emotions as gracefully as I could. Sometimes, I've just been a bitch.

I think what Gabby and I both have had to accept is that we have very different versions of the same childhood. The things I saw as abusive and exploitative, she saw as normal. The memories that stick out for her are not the same ones that trip me up so badly.

One day we got into a fight over some event from our past, and Gabby called me later, crying, "That wasn't my reality, Alexis, maybe that was yours." We've attempted therapy and that didn't work, either. And I've just had to be okay with the fact that we have our own accounts of the same reality.

Just because someone experiences something differently from me doesn't make them right and me wrong, or vice versa. We can all have our own interpretations of the world based on who we are, where we come from, our point of reference on life. And sometimes those experiences are in alignment, and you and I can agree that the sky is blue. But sometimes the temperature will feel hot to one person and cold to another, and both people are still absolutely right in their own experiences. I don't need to convince anyone of my reality anymore. I know what I experienced, and my truth is all that matters for me.

In Buddhism, they talk about "dukkha," the idea that pain is a natural feature of life. We all have it; we have all experienced some level of loss or trauma. The question is: how do we move through it?

I have realized that between my kids, my husband, my family, our work at Alo House, my work as a doula and now my podcast, I just don't have time for people who aren't willing be as "in it" as I am. And I don't mean that in a mean way. It's not that everyone needs to have a master's degree in inspiration. But for me to spend this precious gift of time with you, you at least have to have the willingness to try to get real.

I remember when I got sober, I wanted to have all these friends and get invited to all the parties. I still wanted to be the life of the party and I still am (just ask Evan) but that's not what's important to me. Getting married and having kids absolutely changed what I think is important, and what relationships I am willing to have in my life.

One of the biggest lessons I have learned from Evan—we don't give up on people, but we also don't go down with them. He's an empath like me, and feels deep compassion for people, but he knows he can't save everyone. That that's not his job, and at the end of the day, their stuff isn't really his stuff. For so long, I thought helping people meant you needed to be dragged into their drama, but we can't help people there.

We need to meet them in the middle.

The window for change opens when we get out of the drama and step into the truth. The truth of our own experience, the truth of our own relationships, the truth of who we are when we enter the nothingness. When we truly surrender to the light inside and not all the distractions around us. Then, we can begin to shift our role in the world. And with that, our relationships with the people we love most.

This year, I have been dedicated to shifting my relationship with my husband. Last year, I hit a new bottom: there was a mass shooting in my neighborhood, my grandfather killed himself and then the Woolsey fire destroyed five of the six homes that made up Alo House Malibu. I didn't know how to get out of bed. I realized that every time that had happened to me in sobriety, when I slipped into a depression, I used

Evan to get better. I used him to feel safe. And though he has always been down for the job, I don't want to rely on someone else to be safe anymore. I want to be able to rely on myself and my inner knowingness.

I began a new journey in self-seeking—how do I become the woman I want to be? How do I show up for myself? My children? My family? My partner? How do I stand on my own, not because I have to, not because there is no one there to protect me (because now, finally, there is), but because I am strong and solid and mature enough now to protect myself.

I am no longer ashamed of who I am, and that is a really new feeling for me. When I first had my babies, I joined a number of mom groups on social media. I was literally chased off of one of them by a woman who would follow me from one virtual mom's group to another, blasting to anyone who would listen that I was a felon, a convicted burglar and a drug addict.

It worked. I got kicked out of the group and retreated to my shame.

When we moved to our current neighborhood, I was deathly afraid that someone would expose me and publicly shame me like that again, and that I would be shunned by all our neighbors. I wanted my history to go away so badly. I never really understood and felt in my heart what Evan meant when he would say that my mom and I shouldn't clear my name. He knew that one day I would be able to use my story, the whole story, for good.

But it took a new spiritual teacher, Uta, to show me who I really am, and how to integrate all those different parts of myself—mom, drug addict, burglar, healer, former reality star and everyday person just trying to live in reality—into one.

I'm still getting there. But I now know how to make myself safe, that the drama has to stop with me, and the truth must be told, right now.

## Chapter Seventeen

# Recovering from Reality

*"Not every story has a happy ending...but the discoveries of science, the teachings of the heart, and the revelations of the soul all assure us that no human being is ever beyond redemption. The possibility of renewal exists so long as life exists. How to support that possibility in others and in ourselves is the ultimate question."*
— Gabor Maté

Hi, everyone! *"This is Alexis Neiers calling."*

I know that no matter what I do in life, that voicemail will always be with me. The thing is, for a long time, I was embarrassed by the things that happened to me. I was embarrassed by my sexual molestation, I was embarrassed by my mom, I was embarrassed by Tess and my friends, I was embarrassed by my drug use, I was embarrassed by *Pretty Wild* and I was embarrassed by myself.

I would get this terrible feeling in the pit of my stomach that felt like panic and pain all at once. I lived in shame, which is really just the clinical term for embarrassment. It stemmed from the idea that I was less-than, and not worthy—that I was damaged and no one could fix me. Depression happens when we don't believe that things will get better. And what I discovered was, all that embarrassment led me to believe that things would always be that way. So I thought I could survive only by hiding from life.

I had to start finding other ways to heal. And what I realized was, I had to start embracing my embarrassment. I had to turn embarrassment into empowerment. Because the shit that happened to me wasn't because I was less than, or unworthy, or damaged. It happened to me because hurt people hurt me. And instead of hiding from reality, I could begin sharing that reality with other people who might be able to relate to it somehow. I could start owning my story, but even better, I could use it as a tool for good, to help others.

When I was growing up, I was terrified of school. I felt that I was dumb because I just didn't get it and I couldn't keep up. The hardest part was, I knew I wasn't dumb. I saw the world through my own lens, and maybe it didn't look like everyone else's, but that was a good thing. I think so much of our education system is set up to make children conform. We expect them to learn the same, and act the same, dress the same and behave the same.

And when a child doesn't neatly fit into one of the molds we create for them, they're tossed to the bottom of the class. They become the problem child, the bad student. Today, my nightstand is regularly stacked with books. I feel like I am still catching up on everything I missed in school, growing up.

Getting sober has been so much about reparenting myself.

And part of that was learning to love education. I discovered how to learn from other people, and I don't know that I would be alive today if not for the doctors and therapists, the healers and the helpers that welcomed me to this path of self-exploration.

According to my ACE score, I should be dead by now. As Johann Hari explains in his book, *Chasing the Scream*, you're statistically 4,600 percent more likely to become an IV drug user if you scored a six. Really, the numbers were always stacked against me. And for young people today, that trauma is only compounded by the complicated society we live in. I don't know that I would have survived my teen years if we had social media the way we do now.

I mean, we had Myspace, but nobody knew how to be mean on it yet.

The shit people say about me and my family, even my sweet girls, on Instagram is horrific. Don't get me wrong. There are tons more loving and supportive and amazing people that I have met through social media, but it's like the old 80/20 rule. Eighty percent of the world is loving and supportive and amazing. The other 20 percent pretty much sucks. Social media exposes that 20 percent. It amplifies their voices. And those mean words that make us feel like we aren't worth anything are blasted across social media at top volume to young women and men every day.

And so I wanted to be a voice for a different message. Trauma happens to everyone: divorce, financial stress, abuse in all its forms, parents with mental health problems, addiction and alcoholism, the death of a loved one, unattuned parents. So why aren't we talking about it? When I started to fall apart again last year, I knew it was my time to rise out of the depression that threatened to turn on me every morning, and instead, step into my empowerment. Instead of feeling defeated, I created my podcast, Recovering from Reality, and decided to finally sit down and write this book.

I wanted to create a space where women (and men) could celebrate the raw and radical stories of waking up to their real selves. So many people have shared with me that I helped them to finally start talking about what happened to them.

Ultimately, I think that's what being "woke" is all about. It's not about cancel or call-out culture. It's not about censorship or political correctness, or somehow taking us to a place where we're afraid to speak. It's about waking up to the inequities and privilege and melting polar ice caps that make every day on this planet, as absolutely miraculous as it is, also fucking terrifying. It's a bell that's ringing, calling us to be our own heroes and heroines. And to reach out to our brothers and sisters to hopefully help them in our own small way. Because, after all, that's the whole point of being here, to help and enjoy each other and this beautiful planet.

And staying awake is a full-time job, which is why I wanted to create a community for growing your consciousness. From broken places to badges of honor, I wanted to start with honest conversations about what it looks like to live authentically and define *your* version of thriving, in all its varied glory, whatever it might look like for you.

I was recently listening to Seth Rogan on *The Howard Stern Show*. When Howard asked Seth if he was a weed addict, Seth shared something I feel every day. Life has simply gotten too hard. The world has become so much more complicated and stressful than our brains were built to manage, and just as civilizations have done for centuries, we use plant medicine to manage those stresses.

Using alcohol or drugs doesn't make everyone an addict.

We all have to find ways to cope.

Because if there's one thing I understand, it's why people do drugs. So being sober isn't a requirement to be a part of this club. I just happen to be a recovering woman and mom and wife going through my shit in public.

And I'm inviting you to join me, to go through it together.

Life happens to everyone. And if you're living yours, chances are you've got some bruises. We live in a world that values prisons over people; where man-children make laws about women's bodies; and where healing pain is a for-profit enterprise. Whether you're on the road to recovery, seeking self-care techniques for surviving the capitalist machine, or just need a moment to remember that you're not alone in your loneliness, I want you to know; your trauma doesn't define you. Your decision to deal with it does. Because if this bitch did it, so can you.

The podcast grew out of the pain of living in our New World Order, a place where children can be brutally separated from their parents, where we laugh at other people's pain, where self-care and spirituality can easily become a tool for bypassing the dirty work of healing. And so I wanted a platform to celebrate the humans who are doing the deep soul excavations, whose findings we can so benefit from and be inspired by.

Since launching, what I've been learning is that we are all works in progress, we are all recovering from reality, even the people we don't agree with or don't understand. We're all experiencing the consequences of our collective trauma. It's just some of us don't know what to do with it.

Dr. Gabor Maté asks, "Not why all the addiction, but why all the pain?"

I don't want to live in pain anymore—or at least not in unnecessary suffering—and I don't want to pass down that unprocessed rage and grief I grew up with to my girls. I want to create a healthy and happy family who can move forward and build a better world than our parents left to us.

Like I famously said, maybe, "I wanna lead a country one day for all I know." And fuck it, who knows, maybe I will.

I kid. The truth is, I just want to be a leader for my family. I just want to be an advocate for all. I just want to be a friend to myself. I want to wake up, and look at the woman in the mirror, and know she is so deep in her truth that her mortal body could disappear tomorrow and she would still walk in faith. I want to know that no matter where I go or what happens, that I always see the light that moves through each of us, and ultimately, that connects us to one another.

My favorite moments on this planet are when I get to be present for someone else's birth experience. Because when you hear that first wail, when you hear the parents' response, you know why we are here. We are here to love.

No matter what that love looks like. And though I grew up in anger, doubt and self-hatred, I have found that there is nothing more liberating and powerful than radical love.

I never could have planned this journey, but it's really hard to see the view from the mountaintop when you live in the valley. It's hard to understand the depth and breadth of your life when you're moving through it. And when you're in trauma, when you're in addiction, when you're standing in the middle of Orlando Bloom's living room, totally confused, you can't see how any of that might fit into a bigger picture.

As I said, last year I hit a new bottom, and I knew I needed help finding my way out. So I searched Yelp for a local Reiki healer, and the Universe (and Yelp!) sent me Uta. Over the last year, she helped me to become grounded, to connect deeper with myself and to better negotiate and live more deeply in all my feelings, both the joy and the pain.

Recently, while speaking with her, I asked her why something terrible had just happened.

She replied, "Alexis, we don't ask, 'Why?' We ask, what is being shown to me?"

And I realized that "why" is the place where we hide our feelings. If I can blame you, or my family, or the President of the United States, I don't have to walk through the real lesson of a given circumstance. Evan and I were talking about faith recently. How when we were finally struck sober, we learned to let go and let the power of the Universe sweep over us. We used to swim against the stream, struggling, exhausting ourselves. Instead, we finally stopped, put our arms out, and let the flow carry us where it would, somehow knowing that everything would be okay.

In that same way, we don't have to ask why. We just need to recognize the next right action. We can either respond with fear, or we can respond with love. Because what we realized is that you can have faith, but without radical love, it won't last long. Faith is not a destination, it's the starting point. It's just the part where we let go of the outcome.

Of course, we still must take the action.

We trust in something bigger than ourselves, and we begin to trust ourselves to make decisions and move forward. And out of that action, we build the connections that transform all of our relationships, we build the connections that heal trauma, addiction, and even that scared little girl who hid from herself and the world for so long.

It's that radical, unconditional love that we need to start offering ourselves and each other. That's how we heal. That's how we recover from reality.

And so it is.

# About Alexis Haines

Alexis Haines was once a reality star, heroin addict and member of the "Bling Ring," a group of Hollywood burglars whose exploits became the basis of a Sofia Coppola movie—and for which she served time. Today, she is a mother, wife, writer and birth doula. She and her husband run the addiction treatment center Alo House Recovery Centers, where she inspires young women to tap into their inner knowingness to find empowerment and connection with themselves and others.

She also hosts the raw and resonant Recovering from Reality podcast, a show for people who would rather "wake the fuck up" than fall victim to their own stories. Alexis turns her pain and her most embarrassing moments into opportunities for empowerment and shows others how to do the same.

Alexis has appeared on *Entertainment Tonight, E! News* and *The Doctors* as well as in the pages of *Vice, Us Weekly* and *The New York Post*. She lives in suburban Los Angeles with her husband, two daughters, a cat and a three-legged dog named Sailor—and she can't believe that's where she ended up either.

Made in the USA
Middletown, DE
22 February 2020

85152707R00123